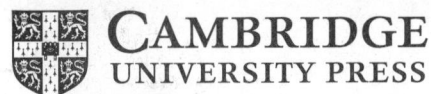

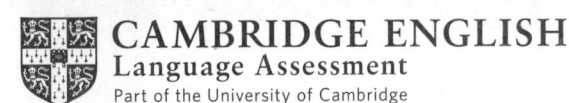

CAMBRIDGE
UNIVERSITY PRESS

CAMBRIDGE ENGLISH
Language Assessment
Part of the University of Cambridge

Cambridge English

CAMBRIDGE OFFICIAL PREPARATION MATERIAL

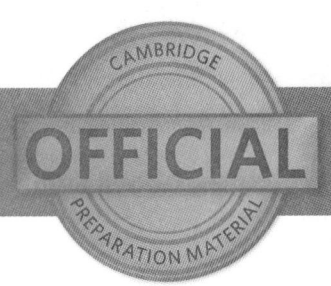

David McKeegan
Series Editor: Annette Capel

# Prepare!

WORKBOOK

Level 7

**Cambridge University Press**
www.cambridge.org/elt

**Cambridge English Language Assessment**
www.cambridgeenglish.org

Information on this title: www.cambridge.org/9780521180382

© Cambridge University Press and UCLES 2015

This publication is in copyright. Subject to statutory exception
and to the provisions of relevant collective licensing agreements,
no reproduction of any part may take place without the written
permission of the publishers.

First published 2015
5th printing 2016

Printed in Italy by Rotolito Lombarda S.p.A.

*A catalogue record for this publication is available from the British Library*

ISBN 978-0-521-18036-8 Student's Book
ISBN 978-1-107-44089-0 Student's Book and Online Workbook
ISBN 978-1-107-49800-6 Student's Book and Online Workbook with Testbank
ISBN 978-0-521-18039-9 Teacher's Book with DVD and Teacher's Resources Online
ISBN 978-0-521-18042-9 Class Audio CDs
ISBN 978-1-107-49798-6 Presentation Plus DVD-ROM

Downloadable audio for this publication at www.cambridge.org/PrepareAudio

The publishers have no responsibility for the persistence or accuracy of URLs
for external or third-party internet websites referred to in this publication, and
do not guarantee that any content on such websites is, or will remain, accurate
or appropriate. Information regarding prices, travel timetables, and other factual
information given in this work is correct at the time of first printing but the
publishers do not guarantee the accuracy of such information thereafter.

# Contents

| | | |
|---|---|---|
| 1 | Creative minds | 4 |
| 2 | Addicted to fashion | 8 |
| 3 | All in the mind | 12 |
| 4 | Take a deep breath | 16 |
| 5 | Past times | 20 |
| 6 | Strong emotions | 24 |
| 7 | Telling stories | 28 |
| 8 | A great place to live | 32 |
| 9 | Being positive | 36 |
| 10 | Surprise! | 40 |
| 11 | The family unit | 44 |
| 12 | Making a difference | 48 |
| 13 | Leading the way | 52 |
| 14 | Getting there | 56 |
| 15 | The bigger picture | 60 |
| 16 | New and improved! | 64 |
| 17 | Making headlines | 68 |
| 18 | Start up | 72 |
| 19 | Points of view | 76 |
| 20 | Speak up | 80 |

# 1 Creative minds

## VOCABULARY  Online, films, music, media

**1 Complete the crossword, using the clues below.**

**Across**

2 a webpage where people regularly record their activities and thoughts
7 give your opinion in a report about a book, film, etc.
8 a group of books or TV programmes about the same topic
10 write a piece of music
12 a work of art that has been popular for a long time and is considered high quality
13 begin a band or other organisation
14 the music for a film or TV programme

**Down**

1 a part of a film or book in which events happen in one place
3 the words of a song
4 a person in a film, play or story
5 all the actors in a film, play or show
6 a popular book which a lot of people buy
9 the sounds we make when we speak or sing
11 put something on a website, e.g. a comment

**2 Complete the sentences with the words in the box.**

| critics   director   editor   novelist   TV presenter |

1 I thought it was a great film, but I read the reviews and the ............................ didn't like it.
2 A ............................ writes books about imaginary people and events.
3 When the ............................ had finished work on the book, it was shorter and better.
4 The company are looking for a young ............................ to host their new talk show.
5 Stephen Spielberg is a famous ............................ who has made a lot of great films.

**3 Find the odd word out.**

| 1 | novelist | blog | director | critic |
| 2 | soundtrack | compose | form | post |
| 3 | lyrics | series | charts | editor |
| 4 | classic | bestseller | cast | version |
| 5 | soundtrack | voice | version | lyrics |
| 6 | charts | character | cast | scene |

## READING

### EXAM TIPS

**Reading and Use of English Part 7**
- Always read the questions first and underline the main ideas in them.
- Read all the texts quickly for general meaning.
- Scan the texts for information that matches the ideas you have underlined in 1–10.
- If you find it easier, concentrate on one text at a time and answer the questions that relate to it.

**1 You are going to read five reviews of fantasy novels. Before you read, underline the main idea in each question.**

**Which book**

| is probably too frightening for young readers? | 1 |
| is about regaining something that has been lost? | 2 |
| contains an element of humour? | 3 |
| involves a journey into the past? | 4 |
| features a character who may be hiding something? | 5 |
| is being turned into a film? | 6 |
| has a main character who is not very sociable? | 7 |
| is one of a series of novels? | 8 |
| takes some ideas from another work? | 9 |
| includes a character interested in magic and games? | 10 |

**2 For questions 1–10, choose from the reviews (A–E). The reviews may be chosen more than once.**

**3 Read the reviews again and underline the parts of the text which give you each answer.**

### A Stitch in Time by Penelope Lively

Maria is always lost in her own little world in which she prefers to chat with animals, trees, plants and inanimate objects, rather than other human beings. But while on holiday she begins to hear things that others can't, and she's not sure what is real any more. Then she finds a nineteenth-century sewn picture and she feels a strange connection with Harriet, the girl who sewed it. As Maria becomes more involved in Harriet's world, she begins to fear that something sad has happened. This book is a gentle, funny and mysterious read from an author who started her career writing film scripts.

### Ante's Inferno by Griselda Heppel

Adults will have heard of Dante's *Inferno* and the author says she was inspired to write her book drawing on the *Inferno*'s riches. Ante and her enemy at school, Florence, plus a boy who has been trapped in the music room for a hundred years, fall into a tunnel leading to the Underworld. There they find themselves in a dark and nightmarish place where characters from Greek mythology exist alongside terrifying, monstrous beings. Their horrifying journey and need to get back to the real world is full of exciting events. While it may be a bit much for pre-teens to deal with, more mature readers will keep turning the pages to find out what dreadful thing is going to happen next.

### The Girl Who Fell Beneath Fairyland and Led the Revels There by Catherynne M. Valente

This is the second breathtaking adventure for September, the strange girl who returns to Fairyland to find that the fairy creatures are in trouble. For a while now they have been losing their shadows and, with their shadow, their magic is disappearing. September learns that it is all to do with a conflict with Fairyland-Below, a dark place where there is no law, and terrifying creatures live. It is a place that September knows she has to visit in order to get back the shadows from the thieves, and to sort out the mess that Fairyland is in. It takes her on an incredible journey that is sometimes dangerous, sometimes terrifying, but always fascinating. Readers young and old will have great fun with this one.

### The Deadly Trap by Jan Burchett & Sara Vogler

Young hero Sam is taken back 300 years onto his favourite pirate ship, the *Sea Wolf*, where the pirates are planning to steal some English gold. Within minutes he meets the new shipmate, Dick, who Sam suspects is not all he claims to be. The other pirates all like him, but Sam is not so sure and sets a trap that Dick falls into, but the others refuse to believe it, going ahead with their piracy plans involving Dick. Sam and his close friend Charlie have to find a way to stop Dick's plan. This is a fast-moving tale, which brings to mind the old-fashioned adventure stories of such classic writers as Stevenson and Defoe.

### Shadow Spell by Caro King

When Nina is set the task to stop the evil Mr Strood from killing the dying land of Drift, she has to find Simeon Dark, the last surviving king and his mansion, for he is the only one who can make sure she is successful. But with Dark's love of tricks, strange creatures and monsters – good and bad – in the way, Nina has a hard mission before her. Readers watch the hero survive a series of thrilling adventures, and fall in love along the way. The book is written for the teen market, but there is nothing unsuitable for younger readers in here. In fact, the movie rights have already been sold to a family-friendly Hollywood production company, and it is due for release next year.

---

**EP Word profile *not***

**Choose the correct answer.**

1 Mario is a great singer and songwriter, not … a very generous man.
 a to mention   b quite   c even

2 Unfortunately, the film wasn't … as good as the critics said it was.
 a only   b half   c to mention

3 I'll be there in a minute – I'm not … ready yet.
 a half   b only   c quite

4 This novel is not … exciting, but also very educational.
 a half   b only   c quite

5 Fascinating? I don't think so. The book isn't … interesting!
 a quite   b half   c even

# GRAMMAR  Simple, continuous or perfect

**1** Choose the correct verbs.

1 **A:** How many films *did you see / have you seen* since the festival started?
   **B:** Three. I *saw / 've seen* the best one yesterday.
2 **A:** We *go / 're going* on holiday to Spain every year.
   **B:** I *never went / 've never been* to Spain.
3 **A:** Hi Tim. What *do you do / are you doing* at the moment?
   **B:** I *do / 'm doing* my English homework.
   **A:** Oh. I *did / 've done* mine yesterday.
4 **A:** *Did you enjoy / Were you enjoying* the concert last night?
   **B:** No, we were too late. When we arrived, the show *finished / had finished*. Nobody *was / has been* there!
5 **A:** What *did you do / were you doing* when I called you last night?
   **B:** I *read / was reading* my favourite writer's new novel. I *read / 'm reading* it now too.
   **A:** Oh, *do you enjoy / are you enjoying* it?
   **B:** Yes, I *love / am loving* her work.

**2** Complete the email with the correct form of the verb in brackets.

Hi Emily
I ¹............................ (write) this email from a café in Edinburgh.
The sun ²............................ (shine), and it's a beautiful day.
Every year we ³............................ (come) to the arts festival here.
It ⁴............................ (be) an annual treat for us since 2010, when we
⁵............................ (move) to Scotland. We usually ⁶............................
(stay) for a week, and go to see as many shows as we can. Last year we
⁷............................ (see) twelve.
One evening last year when we ⁸............................ (walk) back to our
hotel, a group of people dressed as monkeys ⁹............................ (run)
into the road and ¹⁰............................ (start) dancing. It was a very
funny sight, but strange things like that often ¹¹............................
(happen) during the festival.
Another unusual thing ¹²............................ (happen) last night
when we ¹³............................ (sit) in the hotel restaurant. We
¹⁴............................ (just /pay) the bill and we ¹⁵............................ (get)
ready to leave when a journalist with a film crew ¹⁶............................
(come) in and ¹⁷............................ (start) interviewing people. My
brother made us all leave quickly because he ¹⁸............................ (not
want) to be on TV!
Anyway, my friends ¹⁹............................ (just /come) into the café, and
they ²⁰............................ (want) me to go and see a film with them.
Write soon!
Donna

**3** 👁 Correct the mistakes in these sentences or put a tick (✔) by any you think are correct.

1 I had taken so long to write to you because I have been busy. ............................
2 Did you had a good time on your holiday? ............................
3 She has been my best friend since last summer. ............................
4 By the time I arrived, he has disappeared. ............................
5 Surfing is my hobby since 2010. ............................
6 We're having a great time here in London. ............................

# VOCABULARY  Spelling

All except two of these words are misspelled. Correct the mistakes.

1 enviroment   ............................
2 succesful    ............................
3 beleive      ............................
4 choise       ............................
5 especially   ............................
6 althought    ............................
7 untill       ............................
8 necessary    ............................

Unit 1

## WRITING  An essay (1)

See Prepare to write box, Student's Book page 13.

**1** Your teacher has asked you to write an essay on the following subject. Make some notes below about points 1 to 3.

> Young people today want to be rich and famous as a result of watching reality TV and talent shows, but they should have more realistic ambitions. Do you agree?
>
> **Notes**
> Write about:
> 1 your opinion of reality TV and talent shows
> 2 their negative effects on young people
> 3 ................................... (your own idea)

1 ....................................................................
2 ....................................................................
3 ....................................................................

**2** Here are the first two paragraphs of the essay. Do they contain any of your ideas? Read them and check. (Ignore the gaps.)

> Reality TV and talent shows are not exactly educational, but ¹................ that they are not intended to be; they are just for entertainment. I do not believe they are very entertaining either. ²................ , they are extremely popular, especially among young people. The question is, are they really such a bad influence? Some people say they are. ³................ , many teachers have noted that their students have unrealistic ideas about their future. They just want to be rich and famous. ⁴................ , some young people do not care about their schoolwork because they believe you don't need qualifications to be a pop star!

**3** Complete the text with the expressions in the box.

> For instance    Furthermore
> However    most people agree

### EXAM TIPS

**Writing Part 1 (an essay)**
- Make a plan for your essay before you write it.
- Give each paragraph a clear function, for example, an introduction with your opinion, ideas for the statement in the question, ideas against the statement, and a conclusion.
- Use linking words to join your ideas.

**4** Complete the plan with notes from the box below. For 2, use the text in exercise 2.

1 Introduction
....*not educational or entertaining*....................

2 Paragraph 2 – the negative effects of the shows
....................................................................

3 Paragraph 3 – another angle
....................................................................

4 Conclusion – sum up the points
....................................................................

> another idea of your own
> ~~not educational or entertaining~~
> stop caring about schoolwork
> summary of the points made
> unrealistic ideas about the future
> very popular
> very relaxing viewing
> your conclusion

**5** Now complete the essay, using the plan and your notes from exercise 4. Try to use the following linkers in your paragraphs: *to sum up, in contrast*. Write about 70–80 words.

Creative minds 7

# 2 Addicted to fashion

## VOCABULARY  Adjective + preposition

**1** Complete the table with the correct adjectives.

> addicted   adventurous   aware   ~~bothered~~   cautious   critical
> decisive   hopeless   impressed   jealous   loyal   mean

| about | at | by | of | to | with |
|---|---|---|---|---|---|
| bothered | | | | | |
| | | | | | |
| | | | | | |
| | | | | | |

**2** Choose the correct answer.

1 I'm ....... to playing computer games.
  a addicted     b loyal       c adventurous
2 I'll organise the show, because Tara is ....... at making arrangements.
  a impressed    b decisive    c hopeless
3 Dan thought he had written a good essay, but the teacher was very ....... of it.
  a aware        b critical    c jealous
4 She wears expensive clothes, but I'm not ....... by that.
  a impressed    b mean        c adventurous
5 Don't be ....... about your brother's new haircut – he's embarrassed enough!
  a jealous      b mean        c loyal
6 Are you ....... of the risks involved in this plan?
  a aware        b jealous     c critical
7 I'm very ....... about spending a lot of money on the latest fashions.
  a addicted     b adventurous c cautious
8 He's very ....... to a particular brand of clothes – he never wears anything else.
  a critical     b loyal       c adventurous

**3** Read about these young people's attitudes to fashion. Complete the sentence about each one with a phrase from the box.

> addicted to   adventurous with   bothered about
> decisive about   jealous of

1 Meral always buys a new pair of shoes when she has any spare money – she can't stop buying shoes!
  Meral is ................................. buying shoes.
2 Andrea doesn't care what's in fashion.
  Andrea isn't ................................. fashion.
3 Max is happy to try every new fashion idea that comes along.
  Max is ................................. fashion.
4 Anna really doesn't like it when her best friend buys all the new fashions.
  Anna is ................................. her best friend.
5 When he's shopping for clothes, Peter always makes his mind up very quickly.
  Peter is ................................. clothes.

## READING

**1** Look at the picture illustrating the text on page 9. Why do you think sunglasses are always in fashion?

**2** Read the text quickly. Choose the best title.
  a The item that's never out of fashion
  b Why celebrities wear sunglasses
  c How to make money in the fashion business

**3** Read the text again and choose the correct answers.
1 Sunglasses became popular in the *first / twentieth / twenty-first* century.
2 The public didn't buy many sunglasses at first because they were *too expensive / poorly designed / not very effective.*
3 The writer thinks film stars wore sunglasses in order to *show they were famous / protect their eyes from lights / hide their eyes.*
4 The writer thinks that celebrities *wear sunglasses too much / get paid to wear sunglasses / encourage the public to wear sunglasses.*
5 Sunglasses remain popular because they *provide protection / look good / are cheap.*

Unit 2

Can you think of an item which has never been out of fashion, ever since the time it came on the market? You might think denim jeans are a likely candidate. But, while they have always been popular, there have also been times when they were considered to be unfashionable by expert 'fashion watchers'. No, the only fashion item that has always been cool to wear since the start of the twentieth century is … a pair of sunglasses, or 'shades'.

So where did these remarkable things come from? Back in 60 CE the Roman emperor Nero was reported to enjoy watching fighting in the Colosseum through clear green stones to reduce strong light from the sun. Such luxuries were not for everyone, of course. It wasn't until nearly two thousand years later that coloured glasses became cheap and available to the general public.

One of the things that led them to become such desirable fashion items was their popularity with American film stars in the early 1900s. It is commonly believed that this was to avoid being recognised by fans. However, an alternative explanation is that film actors often had red eyes in those days, because of the high-powered lamps that were used in film studios. Whatever the reason, when businessman Sam Foster began selling inexpensive, mass-produced sunglasses in 1929, he found a ready market.

Nowadays they are big business, with hundreds of different brands to choose from. In fact, the industry generates 34 billion dollars per year in sales. Celebrities continue to be unpaid promoters of the products. Singer Elton John, for example, is thought to have a sunglasses collection of over 1,000 pairs. Sunglasses have even played minor roles in films. In the 1999 sci-fi thriller *The Matrix*, starring Keanu Reeves, all the good characters wore round shades, and the bad guys all wore rectangular ones.

But what is the real reason for their continuing popularity? Is it simply the fact that the general public have a strong desire to copy the rich and famous? The truth of the matter is, people wear them for various reasons: comfort and clear vision in bright sunlight, protection against the dangerous rays from the sun, to avoid eye contact with others, or even to hide their emotions. All of these are reasonable excuses for putting on the dark shades. But it is generally recognised that the main reason is much simpler: they look cool!

**4 Find words in the text which mean the following:**

1 having a lot of knowledge and skill (paragraph 1) ........................
2 make less (paragraph 2) ........................
3 expensive things that give pleasure (paragraph 2) ........................
4 wanted by most people (paragraph 3) ........................
5 prevent (paragraph 3) ........................
6 creates (paragraph 4) ........................
7 pleasant, relaxed condition, with no pain (paragraph 5) ........................
8 feelings (paragraph 5) ........................

### Word profile *point*

**Complete the second sentence so that it has a similar meaning to the first sentence, using the word in brackets.**

0 When she spoke about fashion, she said some interesting things. (points)
   She made ...*some interesting points*... when she spoke about fashion.

1 In a limited way, the medicine helped me feel better, but didn't cure me. (up)
   The medicine helped me feel better ........................, but didn't cure me.

2 It's useless trying to persuade him to stop buying new clothes. (no)
   There ........................ trying to persuade him to stop buying new clothes.

3 You didn't understand the main idea of this article. (missed)
   You ........................ of this article.

4 Please hurry up and say what you want to say. (get)
   Please hurry up and ........................ point.

5 I'd love to come to the fashion show but, unfortunately, I'm at work that day. (the)
   I'd love to come to the fashion show but, ........................, I'm at work that day.

Addicted to fashion

## GRAMMAR  Present perfect (continuous)

**1** Choose the correct verb forms.

1. It's time you changed your shirt. You've *worn / been wearing* it for three days!
2. I've *lost / been losing* my new sunglasses.
3. Her skin is red because she's *sunbathed / been sunbathing* without sunscreen.
4. How long have you *studied / been studying* fashion?
5. We've *sold / been selling* six of these dresses today.
6. I've *read / been reading* his latest book, but I'm not enjoying it.
7. You haven't *eaten / been eating* much of your lunch today.
8. They've *drunk / been drinking* coffee since they got up this morning.

**2** Complete the postcard with the verbs in brackets in the present perfect or present perfect continuous.

Hi Tom
How are you? I hope you ¹.................................... (keep) busy at college! We're having a great time here. The weather ²..................................... (be) fantastic so far! I ³..................................... (sit) on the beach all morning, watching the world go by. I ⁴..................................... (already/have) a few ideas for new swimming costume designs for next term's fashion project!
Laura and I ⁵..................................... (meet) some interesting people who are staying in the same hotel as us. They ⁶..................................... (be) here for a couple of weeks already, and they ⁷..................................... (do) research for a project about beach fashions. Yes, they're in fashion too, just like us. In fact, they ⁸..................................... (apply) for jobs for the last few months without any luck, but they think that presenting a full design project will help. What a good idea!
Anyway, Laura ⁹..................................... (try) to attract my attention for the past five minutes, so I'd better see what she wants! I think she wants to go for lunch – we ¹⁰..................................... (not eat) anything since breakfast.
Bye for now,
Sally

**3** ⊙ Correct the mistakes in these sentences or put a tick (✔) by any you think are correct.

1. The football team has been playing badly last year. ............................
2. I have been doing gymnastics for more than ten years. ............................
3. Agustina is my best friend since we met in school when we were three years old. ............................
4. I am playing classical guitar for three years. ............................
5. Yesterday I have been hiking for five hours. ............................
6. I have known Marion for ten years now. ............................

## VOCABULARY  Verb + preposition

Complete the email with the prepositions in the box.

> at   for   of   on   with (x2)   without

Hi Jane
I'm writing a quick note to apologise ¹............................ laughing ²............................ your hat yesterday at school. The truth is, it was a really nice hat compared ³............................ mine. I suppose I was jealous of you! Sometimes I just can't cope ⁴............................ people having nicer things than me. It's very childish, I know. I need to get a summer job, because I hate depending ⁵............................ my parents to give me money to buy things, and I really can't do ⁶............................ some new clothes at least once a month! I'm going shopping now. Have you heard ⁷............................ Coco's? It's a new clothes shop in town. Do you want to come with me?
Dani

Unit 2

## LISTENING

**1** Do you like shopping for clothes? Write down one or two good things and bad things about it.

..................................................................................
..................................................................................
..................................................................................
..................................................................................

**2** ▶2 You will hear four short extracts in which teenagers are talking about shopping for clothes. Which speakers like shopping? Write ✔ or ✘.

Speaker

1  Eddie .......     2  Tanya .......

3  Will .......     4  Hannah .......

**3** ▶2 Listen again. Who says these things?

1  I enjoy making independent decisions. ..........................
2  I am different from my friends. ..........................
3  I want to get a job in fashion. ..........................
4  I often buy nothing when I go shopping. ..........................
5  I enjoy meeting with friends. ..........................
6  I try to be as stylish as possible. ..........................
7  I have very little money. ..........................

**4** ▶2 Listen again and complete these phrases from the extracts. Which one expresses a negative attitude?

1  I don't particularly ............................. .
2  I'm really ............................. fashion.
3  We always ............................. to ...
4  It's quite a ............................. for me.
5  What's not ............................. ?

**5** Read the questions about shopping and write your answers. Use phrases from exercise 4 if you can.

1  Do you enjoy going shopping for clothes?
..................................................................................
2  What do/don't you enjoy about it?
..................................................................................
3  Who do you go shopping with?
..................................................................................
4  When do you go shopping?
..................................................................................
5  What kind of things do you usually buy?
..................................................................................

Addicted to fashion  **11**

# 3 All in the mind

## VOCABULARY  Abstract nouns

**1** Write the abstract nouns that are related to these adjectives.

0 believe ......belief......
1 concentrate ..........................
2 creative ..........................
3 determined ..........................
4 lucky ..........................
5 successful ..........................
6 develop ..........................
7 agree ..........................
8 fortunate ..........................
9 natural ..........................
10 intelligent ..........................

**2** Match the nouns you have written in exercise 1 to these definitions.

1 the ability to learn, understand, and think ..........................
2 the ability to produce new and imaginative things ..........................
3 something that you think is true ..........................
4 the ability to focus your mind on something ..........................
5 when people have the same opinion or make the same decision ..........................
6 when someone continues trying to do something difficult ..........................
7 when you achieve what you want to achieve ..........................
8 all the plants, creatures, substances, and forces that exist in the universe ..........................
9 the process of changing into something new ..........................
10 the good (and bad) things that happen to you (two words) ..........................

**3** Complete the sentences with the correct abstract nouns.

1 It is my .......................... that one day we will discover life on other planets.
2 Education should encourage .......................... as well as give students knowledge.
3 Ian's recent novel was a big .......................... – millions of copies were sold.
4 We finally reached an .......................... about how we were going to complete the task.
5 I can't work with the radio on – it disturbs my .......................... .
6 It was pure .......................... that I met Simon in town – we hadn't arranged to meet.
7 The school is spending a lot of time on the .......................... of a new homework marking system.
8 I've always been impressed by my teacher's .......................... – she's the cleverest person I know.

## READING

**1** Look at the photo in the article. What are the animals doing, and why are they doing it?

..................................................................
..................................................................

**2** Now read the article quickly. What kinds of animals are mentioned as showing similar emotions to humans?

..................................................................

### EXAM TIPS

**Reading and Use of English Part 6**
- Read the text quickly for its general meaning.
- Read the sentences A–G carefully and underline important words.
- Also underline pronouns and other possible links between the sentences and the text.
- Look for links in the sentences before and after each gap in the text.

**3** Six sentences below have been removed from the article. There is one extra sentence. Underline the pronouns and other linking words in each of the sentences.

A It seemed to be willing to go hungry rather than see a fellow animal suffer.
B Empathy plays a role in that as it allows us to understand our fellow humans better.
C This fear of strangers will, we believe, protect us from personal danger.
D Other research has shown animals displaying empathy towards other animals and towards humans.
E The usual effect of this kind of behaviour is that it stops crying, shouting and other signs of being upset.
F We assume that people are able to think themselves into the position of another person, even though they may not have personally experienced that person's circumstances.
G They communicate this requirement by crying for attention and to show pain.

# The origins of empathy

Empathy – the ability to imagine what it must be like in someone else's situation – was traditionally thought to be a quality only possessed by human beings. It is an essential part of what it means to be human, to the extent that we are suspicious of anyone who does not show empathy in their behaviour.

Empathy should not be confused with sympathy – caring about another person's problems – which does not necessarily mean that we understand how we would feel in the same situation. To feel empathy is more involved than simply feeling sorry for someone else's troubles. [1] This is not restricted to real life – we read novels, watch television and go to the theatre, and part of our enjoyment comes from understanding the dilemma faced by the characters because we know how we would feel if we were in the same situation. Empathy is essential to the smooth running of society. We create rules, without which society could not work, and we obey them because we can empathise with our fellow citizens.

However, it seems that in fact empathy may not be a quality unique to humans. One study involving children's reactions to adults pretending to be upset – for example, crying or expressing pain – observed that family pets seemed to be reacting as well. [2] Creatures from across the animal kingdom such as bees and whales, as well as domestic pets, display behaviour that suggests they cooperate with and protect each other.

In another study, psychiatrist Jules Masserman and his team conducted an experiment with monkeys in which the monkeys pulled one of two chains that released food. One chain simply released the food, while another gave an electric shock to a second monkey. The first monkey stopped pulling the chain that delivered the shock. [3] This empathetic behaviour was observed in a number of monkeys.

The origin of empathy is probably the need for the young of all animal species to be cared for. [4] Both human and non-human young were more likely to survive if their parents reacted positively to their needs. People and animals alike are social beings and are more likely to survive if they work together.

**4** Choose from the sentences A–G the one which fits each gap (1–6). There is one extra sentence which you do not need to use.

**5** List the words you underlined in exercise 3 and what they refer to. (The numbers refer to those in the text.)

1 ......we...... human beings
   ......they...... another person
2 ..........................................
3 ..........................................
4 ..........................................
5 ..........................................
   ..........................................
6 ..........................................

**6** Find words or phrases in the text with the following meanings.

1 a part of someone's character (paragraph 1) ..................
2 someone who lives in a particular town or city (paragraph 2) ..................
3 unusual and special (paragraph 3) ..................
4 belonging or relating to the house, home or country (paragraph 3) ..................
5 a group of plants or animals that share similar characteristics (paragraph 5) ..................
6 think of someone or something in a particular way (paragraph 7) ..................

### Word profile *smart*

Match the examples of *smart* to the definitions below.
1 I got a new **smart** phone for Christmas. .....
2 You look very **smart** in your new suit. .....
3 This car has a **smart** navigation system. .....
4 Dolphins are very **smart** animals. .....
5 That's a **smart** shirt. .....
6 You have to be **smart** to get an A in maths. .....

a clever
b stylish
c using computer technology

[5] If we help others, we are also helping ourselves and so empathy is sensible and practical.

We do not always display empathy, however. Just as animals react aggressively to unknown creatures from their own or other species, so humans tend to regard people they don't know with suspicion. [6] Our unwillingness to trust anyone unfamiliar is as natural to us as our empathy towards those we know and love.

All in the mind 13

## GRAMMAR  The grammar of phrasal verbs

**1** Complete the table with the phrasal verbs.

> break down   care for   deal with   get on with
> get out of   let down   put off   show off

| without an object | |
| --- | --- |
| separable | |
| inseparable | |
| inseparable three-part | |

**2** Choose the correct answer.

1 Don't pay any attention to Tom. He's just *showing off / showing him off*.
2 It's an important task – you mustn't *put it off / put off it* any longer.
3 I'm sorry to *let down you / let you down* again.
4 Our car *broke down / broke it down* again last week.
5 Who's going to *care for the cat / care the cat for* while you are on holiday?
6 I don't *get my brother on with / get on with my brother* very well.
7 The exam is tomorrow and there is nothing you can do to *get it out of / get out of it*.
8 I really don't have time to *deal with this problem / deal this problem with* at the moment.

**3** Write the words in the correct order.

1 let / down / me / He's / again
 ..................................................
2 your work / Please / with / on / get
 ..................................................
3 you / down / the TV / Can / turn / ?
 ..................................................
4 the mess / up / I'll / in the kitchen / clear
 ..................................................
5 Our aunt isn't well. is / Mum / her / for / caring
 ..................................................

**4** ⊙ Correct the mistakes in these sentences or put a tick (✔) by any you think are correct.

1 It will show of how healthy the students are.
 ..................
2 I guess it will be up to your expectations.
 ..................
3 She look after me since my childhood.
 ..................
4 The youngest people sometimes make show in front of their friends. ..................
5 I'm looking forward to hearing from you in the near future. ..................

## VOCABULARY  Verb + *to* infinitive

### EXAM TIPS

**Reading and Use of English Part 4**
- Read each first sentence carefully and think about its meaning.
- Think of how the key word is commonly used in a phrase or sentence.
- Read your completed second sentence to check that your answer makes sense and has accurate grammar.
- Make sure you have only used a maximum of five words.

● Complete the second sentence so that it has a similar meaning to the first sentence, using the word given. You must use between two and five words, including the word given.

0 She would not obey her boss's orders.
 **REFUSED**
 She *refused to do what* her boss told her.
1 'Please, please help me with my project,' said John to Sara.
 **BEGGED**
 John ............................................. with his project.
2 Children from poor families generally perform badly at school.
 **TEND**
 Children from poor families ............................................. well at school.
3 My teacher made me do extra maths lessons.
 **FORCED**
 My teacher ............................................. extra maths lessons.
4 Shall I prepare something for you to eat this evening?
 **WANT**
 Do ............................................. something for you to eat this evening?
5 'Don't forget that you must hand in your essay, Ellie,' I said.
 **REMINDED**
 I ............................................. in her essay.
6 Making you angry was not my intention.
 **INTEND**
 I ............................................. you angry.

# WRITING  An informal letter or email

See Prepare to write box, Student's Book page 23.

**1** Join the two halves of the informal expressions and write them below.

| 0 | Thanks so much | a | soon. |
|---|---|---|---|
| 1 | Write | b | is, ... |
| 2 | The thing | c | I reckon ... |
| 3 | But don't | d | forget that ... |
| 4 | To start | e | care. |
| 5 | It's lovely | f | with ... |
| 6 | As far | g | for your email. |
| 7 | Keep | h | in touch. |
| 8 | To be honest, | i | happy to ... |
| 9 | I'm very | j | to hear from you. |
| 10 | Take | k | as I know, ... |

0 *g Thanks so much for your email*
1 ............................................
2 ............................................
3 ............................................
4 ............................................
5 ............................................
6 ............................................
7 ............................................
8 ............................................
9 ............................................
10 ............................................

**2** Read the following exam task. How many questions should you answer in your email?

> You have received this email from your English friend, Andy.
>
> > I'm doing a project about people's attitudes to pets around the world. Here in Britain, more than 50% of households have a pet, with dogs being the most popular, followed by cats. What do you think about this? Are pets popular in your country? If so, which kind? I'd really value your opinion.
> > Andy
>
> Write your **email**.

**3** Look at these sentences from an email in response to Andy. Which two sentences should not be in the response? Put a cross (✗) by them.

1 People tend not to keep pets in my country, because most people live in flats. ......
2 People in Britain obviously really love animals! ......
3 I think it's cruel to keep animals in zoos. ......
4 If people keep a pet, it's usually a small animal or bird, like a budgie. ......
5 I don't agree that 50% of British households have a pet. ......
6 It's interesting that dogs are the most popular; they need a lot of attention. ......

**4** Which questions in Andy's email do the correct sentences from exercise 3 answer?

**5** Make notes to answer the following questions.

1 Do you think 50% is a lot of households to have pets?
...........................................................
2 What does that say about British people?
...........................................................
3 Do you have a pet? What do you have?
...........................................................
4 Do you know anyone with a different pet? What?
...........................................................
5 What do you think are the advantages of having a pet?
...........................................................
6 What are the disadvantages of having a pet?
...........................................................

## EXAM TIPS

**Writing Part 2 (an informal letter or email)**
- Answer all the questions or points in the task.
- When you have written your text, check that you have answered everything.
- Check that you have written between 140 and 190 words.
- Remember to use informal language throughout.

**6** Write this reply to Andy's email. Use your answers to exercise 5 and some informal expressions from exercise 1.

> Dear Andy
> Thanks so much for your email. It's lovely to hear from you. ...........................
> ...........................................................
> ...........................................................
> In my country,
> ...........................................................
> ...........................................................
> ...........................................................
> To be honest,
> ...........................................................
> ...........................................................
> ...........................................................
> Take care!

All in the mind  15

# 4 Take a deep breath

## VOCABULARY  Stress

**1** Complete the puzzle, using the clues to help you.

1 It's hard to concentrate when you're going over and over something in your … .
2 Tell Lizzy to lie down – she looks like she's going to … !
3 I need to sit down – I … dizzy.
4 No lunch for me, thanks. I've lost my … .
5 I always get in a … the day before a test.
6 I must have eaten something bad, because I have got an … stomach now.
7 The teacher will … her temper if we are late again.
8 I don't like people who are …, and start shouting at the slightest thing.
Word down (↓): ................................

**2** Complete the sentences with some of the phrases from exercise 1.

1 I couldn't sleep last night because I was ........................................ our argument ........................................ .
2 Jenny had a spicy curry for dinner last night and now she's got ........................................ .
3 My brother kept changing the TV programme and Mum ........................................ and shouted at him.
4 You'll ........................................ if you run round in circles like that!
5 I couldn't find my house key this afternoon and I started to ........................................ .
6 Miss Harrison had to stop the class today because one of the students ........................................ and a doctor came.
7 Dad's back is really bad at the moment and he's ........................................ , so he feels tired all the time.
8 I usually ........................................ when I have a cold because I can't taste anything.

**3** Complete the sentences so that they are true for you.

1 The last time I lost my temper was when ........................................
2 ........................................ gives me an upset stomach.
3 Sometimes I get in a panic when ........................................
4 I lost my appetite when ........................................
5 When I have difficulty sleeping, I ........................................
6 ........................................ makes me feel dizzy.

## READING

**1** Look at the picture of an anechoic chamber on page 17. What do you think it is for? Do you think it is a pleasant or a stressful place to be?
........................................
........................................

**2** Read the text quickly. Did the writer enjoy his experience in the anechoic chamber?
........................................

**3** Now read the text again and answer the questions.

1 What did the anechoic chamber remind the writer of?
........................................
2 Why is the absence of sound upsetting for most people?
........................................
3 Why does the chamber have to be completely dark?
........................................
4 Why did the writer feel that the chamber wasn't silent at all?
........................................
5 What was the main reason for the writer leaving the chamber?
........................................

**4** Read the sentences. Write A if the information is correct, B if it is incorrect or C if the information isn't given.

1 The writer was unhappy because his family annoyed him. ........
2 Orfield Laboratories' anechoic chamber is the quietest place in the world. ........
3 The violinist entered the chamber as part of a training programme. ........
4 The writer felt confident before he entered the chamber. ........
5 People were surprised that the writer stayed in the chamber for so long. ........
6 The writer regularly returns to the chamber at Orfield Laboratories. ........

Unit 4

# The sound of silence

Sometimes all I want is a bit of peace and quiet. When I've got some important homework to finish, and my sister won't stop chatting on her phone; when I'm trying to concentrate on the book I'm reading, and Grandma is watching TV downstairs with the sound on high; or when I just want to catch an extra hour's sleep on a Saturday morning, it seems that all the noises – both inside the house and outside – are doing their best to keep me awake. Too much noise can drive anyone mad!

So last summer I decided to go on a mission to find the quietest place on Earth. To my surprise, I didn't have to travel far. I live in Minnesota, home of the Orfield Laboratories, and the world's best anechoic chamber. An anechoic chamber is a small room, made up of layers of concrete and steel to remove outside noise, much like a standard sound recording studio in many ways. But in this case, even the floor is suspended to stop any sound of footsteps. According to the *Guinness Book of Records*, it's the quietest place on Earth – 99.9% sound-absorbent. The strange thing is that most people find its perfect quiet upsetting. Not being able to hear the usual sounds can be frightening. Astronauts do part of their training in anechoic chambers at NASA, so they can learn to cope with the silence of space.

The fact that you can hear sounds means that things are working; when sound is absent, that signals something is wrong. One violinist tried spending some time in the chamber, and banged on the door after a few seconds, demanding to be let out because he was so disturbed by the silence.

But I was determined to try it, so I collected all my savings and booked a 45-minute session – even though no one had managed to stay in for that long before. I felt anxious for two reasons: would I go crazy and tear off my clothes? Or would I just be disappointed that it wasn't as different as I'd hoped?

When the heavy door closed behind me, I was surrounded by darkness, as lights can make a noise. For the first few seconds, being in such a quiet place felt really cool. I tried hard to hear something and heard … nothing.

Then, after a minute or two, I began to hear the sound of my breathing – so I held my breath. Then my heartbeat seemed to become really loud. As the minutes passed by, I started to hear the blood rushing in my veins. I frowned and heard the skin move over my head, which was very strange. Then I started to feel a bit disappointed – this place wasn't silent at all.

After I while I stopped concentrating on the sounds my body was making and began to enjoy it. I didn't feel frightened, and came out only because my time was up; I would happily have spent longer in there. I'd made it – I'd beaten the record! Can you imagine how impressed everyone was?

My 45 minutes in the anechoic chamber was a really interesting and important experience for me. It made me appreciate the quiet times I have, but more than that – it made me appreciate everyday sounds. My sister still chats on her cellphone, and Grandma still has the TV on too loud – but I don't get so annoyed by them any more.

## Word profile *control*

**Match the examples of *control* to the definitions below.**

1 She could hardly **control** herself when she heard that she'd won the lottery. ........
2 I can't turn this mp3 player down because the volume **control** is broken. ........
3 Please **control** your children when you are in this restaurant. ........
4 We're trying to **control** the amount of traffic we allow in the town centre. ........
5 I'm sorry, I don't have any **control** over what my brother does in his spare time. ........

a make someone or something do what you want
b stay calm
c limit the number or amount of something
d the power to make someone or something do what you want
e a switch or other device used to operate a machine

## GRAMMAR  Modals (1): Necessity and obligation

**1** Read the sentences and choose the correct function of the modal verb.

1  We mustn't forget to do our homework.
   a  prohibition    b  lack of obligation    c  advice
2  You should try to get more sleep every night.
   a  obligation    b  advice    c  prohibition
3  They don't have to wear a uniform.
   a  lack of obligation    b  prohibition    c  necessity
4  Do you really need to play your music so loudly?
   a  prohibition    b  advice    c  necessity
5  You can't stay here!
   a  necessity    b  prohibition    c  lack of obligation
6  I must remember to send Elena a thank-you note.
   a  obligation    b  necessity    c  prohibition
7  We have to finish this project by Monday morning.
   a  obligation    b  advice    c  lack of obligation
8  Getting fit needn't be hard work.
   a  advice    b  lack of obligation    c  prohibition

**2** Choose the correct modal verb to complete the conversations.

1  **A:** Greg was shouting at me again last night.
   **B:** He really *needs / must* learn how to control his temper.
2  **A:** I feel so tired every day.
   **B:** You *ought to / needn't* try to go to bed earlier.
3  **A:** You *don't have to / mustn't* come to the match if you don't want to.
   **B:** Thanks. I'm feeling a bit tired.
4  **A:** I don't feel like doing my English homework tonight.
   **B:** Why? Learning vocabulary *needn't / has to* be boring.
5  **A:** Do you want to come to the cinema tonight?
   **B:** Sorry, I *don't have to / can't*. I stay in on Tuesdays to look after my sister.
6  **A:** It's Dan's birthday tomorrow, isn't it?
   **B:** Oh, yes! I *mustn't / don't have to* forget to buy him a card.
7  **A:** I'm going to England in April.
   **B:** You *need / should* visit the British Museum.
8  **A:** I'm just off to the gym.
   **B:** Don't be late. You know we *mustn't / have to* be up early to catch the train.

**3** ⊙ Correct the mistakes in these sentences or put a tick (✔) by any you think are correct.

1  I had to decide what to buy.
   ..............................
2  I suppose you will must have fun in New York.
   ..............................
3  We can't decide where we should go. ..............................
4  I've been told to give my opinion about whether students only had to study what they enjoy.
   ..............................
5  You only have one life, and you don't have to waste it.
   ..............................

## VOCABULARY  Phrasal verbs: health

Complete the conversation with the correct form of one of the phrasal verbs.

> come down with    cut down on
> get someone down    get over
> pass out    stay up

**Sara:** Hi, Steve. How are you? You look a bit rough.
**Steve:** I don't feel good, Sara. I ¹............................. till one o'clock last night playing computer games.
**Sara:** You play too much! You should try to ²............................. your computer use, especially before bed.
**Steve:** I know! I nearly ³............................. when I stood up at the end of the maths lesson this morning. How are you, anyway? You look great.
**Sara:** Thanks. Actually I have just ⁴............................. a bad case of flu. I was in bed for a week!
**Steve:** Poor you. I hate being ill. It really ⁵............................. me ............................. .
**Sara:** Me too. But you really should sort out your sleep or you'll ⁶............................. something nasty before too long.
**Steve:** I know, I know!

## LISTENING

**1** ▶3 You will hear five extracts in which teenagers are talking about free-time activities. Listen and match the speakers with the photos.

Speaker 1 .......
Speaker 2 .......
Speaker 3 .......
Speaker 4 .......
Speaker 5 .......

**2** Now look at the options in exercise 3. Can you make a note of what each speaker liked most about their activity? If you can't remember, try to guess.

Speaker 1 .............................
Speaker 2 .............................
Speaker 3 .............................
Speaker 4 .............................
Speaker 5 .............................

### EXAM TIPS

**Listening Part 3**
- Read all the options before you listen.
- Try to think of other ways that the ideas might be expressed, as the speakers will use different words from the ones in the options.
- Remember that you will hear the recording twice.

**3** ▶3 ● Listen again and for questions 1–5, choose from the list (A–H) what each speaker likes best about their activity. Use the letters only once. There are three extra letters which you do not need to use.

A meeting new people
B getting fit
C learning new things
D earning money
E socialising with people
F relaxing for the evening ahead
G experiencing a sense of achievement
H dealing with daily problems

Speaker 1 [ ] 1
Speaker 2 [ ] 2
Speaker 3 [ ] 3
Speaker 4 [ ] 4
Speaker 5 [ ] 5

Take a deep breath

# 5 Past times

## VOCABULARY  History

**1** Put the letters in the correct order to make words.

```
0 CATILIVISNIO    civilisation
1 KONGDIM         ..................
2 TRENYCU         ..................
3 THYM            ..................
4 BRITE           ..................
5 DACDEE          ..................
6 ZITNECI         ..................
7 THANBANITI      ..................
8 ROTANECS        ..................
9 CHULAN          ..................
```

**2** Match the words in exercise 1 to the definitions.

- a period of 100 years
- b person who has the right to live in a country
- c group of people living together, usually far from cities
- d country ruled by a king or queen
- e relative who lived a long time ago
- f person who lives in a particular place
- g very old story which is probably not true
- h period of ten years
- i the culture and way of life of a society at a particular time
- j make a new product or service available

**3** Complete the sentences with words from exercises 1 and 2 in the correct form.

1 Great Britain is a ..................... because a king or queen is the head of state.
2 Hercules is a character from a number of Greek and Roman ..................... .
3 The 1990s was the ..................... which saw the rise of the internet.
4 We are living in the twenty-first ..................... .
5 Egyptology is the study of the ancient Egyptian ..................... .
6 She is applying to become a ..................... of the USA.
7 My ..................... came from North Africa.
8 The Zulu is a ..................... in South Africa, with around 11 million people.
9 My favourite writer is going to ..................... a book about ancient history next month.
10 The ..................... of the fishing village cooperated happily with the film-makers.

## READING

### EXAM TIPS

**Reading and Use of English Part 2**
- Read the title to find out what the text is about.
- Read the whole text first before you decide on your answers.
- Look at each gap and decide what type of word is needed – an article, a preposition, a pronoun, a modal verb or something else?

**1** What part of speech is gapped in each of these sentences? Choose from the list below.

1 A circus ....... built in Ancient Rome.   ..b..
2 I came ....... with flu so I missed the performance. .......
3 What's the point ....... going to the circus? .......
4 Come with us. I think that you ....... enjoy it. .......
5 Danny enjoyed the show, but I didn't like ....... . .......
6 ....... Roman Empire fell in the fifth century. .......
7 A ....... of people attended circuses in Egypt. .......
8 They let us in even ....... we were very late. .......

a modal verb
b verb *be*
c pronoun
d phrasal verb
e conjunction
f article
g quantifier
h preposition

**2** Now write the correct word in the gaps in exercise 1.

**3** Read the text about the circus on page 21. Do not try to fill the gaps this time. How many civilisations are mentioned in the text?

..................................................

**4** For questions 1–8, read the text on page 21 and think of the word which best fits each gap. Use only one word in each gap. There is an example at the beginning (0).

**5** The eight words you needed to complete the text are among the words in the box below. Make sure your answers are there!

| another | any | as | at | be | do |
|---|---|---|---|---|---|
| it | like | no | ~~of~~ | other | over |
| to | up | used | were | would | |

20  Unit 5

# The circus
## ORIGINS AND HISTORY

The idea (0) ...of... travelling performers has its origins far back in history. (1) ............ is believed that the Ancient Egyptians had groups of travelling acrobats, and people may have been entertaining each (2) ............ in similar ways even further back in time.

The word *circus* comes from the Ancient Greek and Roman word for 'circle' because acts (3) ............ performed in round arenas. The Ancient Greeks (4) ............ have chariot races, horse shows, staged battles, trained animals, jugglers and acrobats in these places. In the ancient city of Rome there was a fixed building where the shows used (5) ............ take place. The first one to be built was called the Circus Maximus. This stone building could seat (6) ............ many as 200,000 people.

When the Roman Empire fell, these large circus buildings fell out of use. Instead, performers travelled between towns in Europe performing (7) ............ local fairs. Groups of entertainers and acrobats have done this for hundreds of years – and they will probably (8) ............ so for many years to come.

By far the most famous Roman circus building was the Colosseum in Rome, built during the time of the Flavian emperors. Construction of the Colosseum was begun sometime between 70 and 72 CE during the time of Vespasian. It is located just east of the Palatine Hill, on the grounds of what was Emperor Nero's Golden House.

The water was removed from the artificial lake that was the central feature of that palace, and the Colosseum was built there – a decision that was made for largely political reasons. Vespasian, whose path to power had relatively poor beginnings, chose to replace the unpopular Nero's private lake with a public amphitheatre that could hold tens of thousands of Romans.

The structure was officially opened in 80 CE by Titus in a ceremony that included 100 days of games. Later, in 82 CE, Domitian completed the work by adding the top storey. Unlike earlier amphitheatres, which were nearly all dug into convenient hillsides for extra support, the Colosseum is an independent structure of stone and concrete, measuring 189 by 156 metres overall.

The amphitheatre seated around 50,000 spectators, who were protected from the sun by a massive cloth roof called a 'velarium'. Hundreds of Roman sailors were required to pull the ropes that opened and closed this roof! The Colosseum was the scene of thousands of hand-to-hand fights between gladiators, of contests between men and animals, and of many larger battles.

The Colosseum was damaged by lightning and earthquakes in medieval times and, even more severely, by theft and criminal damage. All the seats and decorative materials disappeared, as the site was treated with very little respect for more than 1,000 years. Work to preserve the Colosseum began properly in the nineteenth century, and a project to restore it was started in the 1990s. It has long been one of Rome's major tourist attractions. There are many changing exhibitions relating to the culture of Ancient Rome.

**6** Read the text about the Colosseum and choose the correct answers below.

1. Work on the Colosseum was started by the Roman Emperor *Vespasian / Nero / Palatine*.
2. The Colosseum was built for the benefit of the Roman *people / Emperor / environment*.
3. The roof of the Colosseum was operated by *gladiators / spectators / sailors*.
4. Most of the damage to the Colosseum was caused by *natural disasters / war / people*.

**7** Find words in the text which mean the following.

1. not natural (paragraph 5)   ............................
2. level of a building (paragraph 6)   ............................
3. very seriously (paragraph 8)   ............................
4. very important (paragraph 8)   ............................

### EP Word profile *take*

Choose the correct answer.

1. Clean running water is something we take for ........ .
   a opportunity   b granted   c account
2. I'm going to stay at home and take it ........ today.
   a granted   b easy   c account
3. You need to take into ........ how much sleep you get every night.
   a account   b granted   c opportunity
4. We took the ........ to have a bite to eat.
   a granted   b opportunity   c account

Past times 21

## GRAMMAR  Present and past habits

**1 Choose the correct answer.**

1 When I was younger I *would / used to* love sleeping until 11.00 in the morning.
2 He *eats / is eating* a lot of meat and fish at the moment because he's training for a match.
3 My sister *is constantly looking / constantly looks* for new shoes.
4 When we were at primary school, we *would go / were going* to bed before nine during the week.
5 I always *feel / am feeling* hungry when I wake up in the morning.
6 Daniel *used to / would* be better-looking than he is now.

**2 Complete the sentences using the words in brackets.**

0 Stacey arrives late too often, and it annoys you. (always)
   Stacey ..is..always..arriving..late....
1 When you were a child you rode a tricycle every day. (would)
   When I was a child ............................ .
2 The sofa is your temporary bed while your room is being decorated. (sleeping)
   I ............................ while my room is being decorated.
3 Susan hated shopping for clothes when she was a child. (used)
   When she was a child, Susan ............................ .
4 Going for a run is something you do every morning. (go)
   I ............................ every morning.
5 You get annoyed at yourself because you frequently forget your key. (am)
   I ............................ my key!
6 Your grandfather always used to tell silly jokes when you were younger. (constantly)
   My grandfather ............................ silly jokes when I was younger.

**3 👁 Choose the correct sentence in each pair.**

1 a I use to ride horses when I was young.
   b I used to ride horses when I was young.
2 a I have listened to music since I was five years old.
   b I used to listen to music since I was five years old.
3 a We were going to the same school and every morning she used to come to take me from my house.
   b We were going to the same school and every morning she was coming to take me from my house.
4 a We will remember the good times from the past and have a lovely time, as we used to.
   b We will remember the good times from the past and have a lovely time, as we use to.

## VOCABULARY  Expressing frequency

**1 Find a word or expression in the box below with a similar meaning to these adverbs.**

1 rarely          ............................
2 constantly      ............................
3 occasionally    ............................
4 most days       ............................
5 sometimes       ............................

> all the time    from time to time    often
> once in a while    seldom

**2 Put the adverbs and expressions in brackets in the correct position.**

0 My dad ...constantly... asks me how I'm doing at school ............................ . (constantly)
1 We go ............................ to a circus ............................ . (every once in a while)
2 I ............................ go to bed after midnight ............................ . (seldom)
3 My best friend and I ............................ meet for a chat ............................ . (most weeks)
4 I ............................ read a newspaper ............................ . (every day)
5 I ............................ visit an art gallery ............................ . (from time to time)
6 I ............................ listen to music ............................ . (rarely)
7 My family ............................ eats in a restaurant ............................ . (almost never)
8 ............................ I drink ............................ at least three glasses of water. (most days)

**3 Rewrite the sentences in exercise 3 so that they are true for you.**

0 ...My dad seldom asks me how I'm doing at school.
1 ............................
2 ............................
3 ............................
4 ............................
5 ............................
6 ............................
7 ............................
8 ............................

Unit 5

## WRITING  An article (1)

See Prepare to write box, Student's Book page 35.

**1** Look at the exam task below and think about how you would organise your article. Write these questions and the note into the plan on the right according to where you think the answers fit best.

a summary sentence or two
Who is the person?
What would you ask them?
Why are they famous?
Why would you like to meet them?
What do you admire about them?

> You see this announcement in an international English language magazine.
>
> > **My hero from history**
> > Which person from history do you most admire?
> > What things would you ask him or her if you were able to travel back in time?
> > Write us an article answering these questions.
> > We will publish the best articles in the next issue.
>
> Write your **article**.

**2** The article on the right contains the four paragraphs in exercise 1. Number them in the correct order.

**3** Is the order in the article the same as your plan in exercise 1? Which paragraphs address which parts of the question?

Paragraph 1 ...introduces the person and says why he's a hero....
Paragraph 2 ..................................................
Paragraph 3 ..................................................
Paragraph 4 ..................................................

**4** Read the article again. Is the style formal or informal? Underline the sentences which indicate this.

### EXAM TIPS

**Writing Part 2 (an article)**
- Divide your article into paragraphs.
- Cover each point from the task in a separate paragraph.
- Include a title to suggest what the article is about.
- Use an informal style throughout the article.

**5** Which famous person from history would you like to meet? Use the model in exercise 1 to make notes, then write your own article. Write 140–190 words.

---

**My hero from history**

Paragraph 1 introduction:
..................................................

Paragraph 2:
..................................................

Paragraph 3:
..................................................

Paragraph 4 conclusion:
..................................................

---

........
All in all, I think the world would be a better place if there were more people like Gandhi alive. His non-violence and his ability to bring different people together for a common purpose would help the world become a happier and more peaceful place. Who doesn't want that?

........
Believe me, there are so many questions I would like to ask Gandhi if I could meet him! The main thing I would like to know is what would he do to stop all the wars and fighting in the world today. Does he have a solution?

........
The person from history I would most like to meet is Mahatma Gandhi. He was an Indian politician who died in 1948, and I believe he was a really exceptional man. Not only that – he helped India become an independent nation.

........
I admire him because of his bravery and because of his use of non-violent techniques to achieve his aims. He believed in the power of truth. One of the most amazing things he did was unite people of different religions in India in order to gain independence.

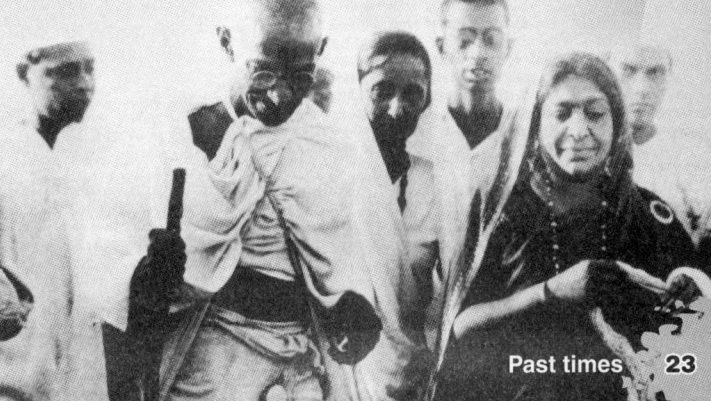

# 6 Strong emotions

## VOCABULARY  Expressing emotions

**1** Match the words and phrases to the definitions below.

1. optimistic ......
2. pessimistic ......
3. over the moon ......
4. furious ......
5. scared ......
6. fed up ......
7. relieved ......
8. depressed ......
9. content ......

a happy that something unpleasant has not happened
b very pleased about something
c very angry
d unhappy and without hope for the future
e frightened
f always believing that bad things are likely to happen
g annoyed or bored by something that you have experienced for too long
h always believing that good things will happen
i pleased with your situation and not hoping for change or improvement

**2** Complete the sentences with words from exercise 1.

1. I always get ............................ when I watch horror films.
2. I was ............................ when I found out my bike had been stolen.
3. I was ............................ about winning first prize in the essay competition.
4. I'm really ............................ with my brother for borrowing my laptop without asking me.
5. He's feeling ............................ about passing his exams tomorrow because he didn't revise much.
6. I'm feeling ............................ about passing my exams because I've done lots of revision.
7. I was ............................ when our lost cat turned up safe and well this morning.
8. I sometimes get ............................ by all the bad news I see on TV.
9. She's a very happy person who is ............................ with her life.

**3** Choose the correct answers. Sometimes two are correct.

1. Our new teacher is really good fun. She's always *bright / depressed / cheerful*.
2. Mum was angry when I got home late last night, but I know that it was because she was *down / concerned / anxious* about me.
3. Jude was a bit *irritated / relieved / content* because I lost her favourite scarf.
4. When my brother wasn't allowed to go on the school trip he got really *content / over the moon / bad-tempered* with our parents.
5. Our cousins have got a huge dog and my little sister was *scared / fed up / petrified* of it when they visited us.
6. I was really *down / bright / depressed* when I failed my maths exam.

**4** Find the odd word out.

1. down        depressed    cheerful     pessimistic
2. irritated   concerned    furious      bad-tempered
3. fed up      relieved     optimistic   over the moon
4. content     cheerful     concerned    relieved
5. furious     petrified    scared       anxious

## READING

**1** Look at the picture. What is the teenager doing?

**2** What does the word *daydream* mean? Try to guess before you look it up in a dictionary.

**3** Read the text quickly. How many 'brain states' does the article talk about? What are they called?

# Happily bored!

Have you ever complained about being bored? Most of us have, without realising how lucky we are! Many people think of boredom as something to be avoided, but being bored can actually lead to great things.

Here is an experiment for you to try. Just do nothing for a moment. Observe your thoughts. Your brain isn't doing nothing, is it? It's listening and watching, processing everything around you, and it may seem quite busy. Your brain is in *Beta mode*. In this state, we act and get things done. Beta brainwaves increase when we are learning, talking or excited, and help us to focus and meet goals. They can also increase stress or make it harder to fall asleep.

Now try being truly bored. Just sit there and relax; clear your mind. Gradually, you may notice that your thoughts become less busy. After a while, you may become aware of the little sounds and events around you. You may begin to think things that had never crossed your mind before. Or you might hardly think at all.

When your brain is this inactive, you are said to be in *Alpha mode*. Alpha waves happen when we are very peaceful or relaxed. Our breathing slows. People who spend more time in this state are more likely to daydream, and tend to fall asleep and stay asleep more easily. They might also get less stuff done!

Scientists use a special electronic device to measure brain activity and they can tell whether the brain is in Alpha or Beta mode. Brainwave activity changes all the time, depending on what we are doing or feeling.

Famous creative thinker Steve Jobs, who co-founded Apple Computers and directed the development of iPads and other new technology, said, 'Boredom allows us to experience curiosity, and out of curiosity comes everything.' He spent many productive hours being bored, and ended up having some pretty amazing ideas.

Scientist Albert Einstein said, 'The monotony of a quiet life stimulates the creative mind.' As a young man, he had a dull job as a clerk in an office. Just imagine him sitting there with nothing to do, twiddling his thumbs and daydreaming. Do you think young Albert would have had the flashes of inspiration which led to his famous theories if he'd had a mobile phone or computer with games on it back in 1903? Or would he have been too busy trying to reach the next stage in his favourite game?

You didn't know daydreaming was a valuable activity, did you? Many large companies, like Google and Pixar Animation, see creativity as a major business advantage and they reward their most creative daydreamers for coming up with original ideas. They even have special rooms for encouraging daydreaming, complete with comfortable sofas. If you work there, you are encouraged to relax and stare into space sometimes, because the companies can see what great ideas come out of these daydreaming sessions.

It can be hard to find the time to be bored. If you are lucky enough to have quiet time or simple, repetitive jobs to do, enjoy those moments of boredom. You might have an inspiration while you are peeling potatoes, or come up with the next brilliant idea for a story while you're watching the rain run down the window. And that's not boring at all, is it?

**4** Are the following statements true or false, or is there no information given in the text?

|   | True | False | Not given |
|---|---|---|---|
| 1 The brain is more active in the Beta state. | | | |
| 2 Some people are always in the same brain state. | | | |
| 3 Steve Jobs was less creative when he was in Alpha state. | | | |
| 4 Albert Einstein had some very good ideas when he was a clerk. | | | |
| 5 Google and Pixar encourage their employees to sleep at work. | | | |
| 6 People should always try to avoid being bored. | | | |

**5** Find the words or phrases in the text which mean the following.

1 give concentrated attention (paragraph 2)
2 thought about something for a short time (paragraph 3)
3 be likely to do something (paragraph 4)
4 the feeling of wanting to know about something (paragraph 6)
5 thinking of an idea (paragraph 8)

Strong emotions

## GRAMMAR  be/get used to

**1 Complete the conversations with the correct form of (not) be/get used to.**

0 A: How's your new job in the café?
  B: It's okay. I didn't like it at first, but I .'m getting used to. it slowly.
1 A: Why has the cat disappeared?
  B: There are too many children in the house, and the cat .................................... it. (not)
2 A: I .................................... getting up so early in the morning. (not)
  B: Don't worry, you .................................... it.
3 A: What do you think of your new teacher, Mrs Smith?
  B: She's nice, but we .................................... having so much homework to do! (not)
4 A: Our kitchen is being redecorated, so we have to eat in a restaurant every night. I .................................... it! (not)
  B: I wouldn't like that. I .................................... eating good home cooking.

**2 Read the situations and complete the sentences using be used to or get used to.**

1 We moved house from the city to the country. It was really quiet at night, which was strange for me. I ..was used to.. hearing the noise of the city when I lay in bed at night. It took me a long time to .................................... the silence.
2 When I started training with the school swimming team, it was hard work. I .................................... so much exercise! My coach told me I would .................................... it quite quickly, but it wasn't true. I've been training for two months and I .................................... it yet!
3 Susan became a vegetarian last year. Her mother was irritated because she .................................... cooking the same meal for the whole family. She didn't want to cook a special meal just for Susan. But, she soon .................................... it. It took Susan a long time to .................................... living without meat, though!

**3 Choose the correct words.**

1 When I was a little girl, I *used to / was used to* have a red skateboard.
2 We don't think we'll ever *be used to / get used to* this cold weather.
3 When I was a child, we *got used to / used to* visit my aunt in the country every spring.
4 I didn't like these new jeans at first, but I *am being / am getting* used to them now.
5 They *used to / are used to* live in the United States.
6 My granddad *doesn't use to / isn't used to* having so many people in the house.

**4 Correct the mistakes in these sentences or put a tick (✔) by any you think are correct.**

1 In Sofia there are subways and trains but people are not used to travel on them. ..................
2 I'm afraid I'll have to bring lots of clothes as I'm not used to living in such a cold place. ..................
3 I can cook very well too, because I use to do doing it when my mother is not at home. ..................
4 I got used to deal with people and I love cooking different kinds of dishes. ..................

## VOCABULARY  Adverbs: type and position

**1 Complete the table with the words from the box.**

definitely   from time to time   however
immediately   in my bedroom   ~~last year~~
nevertheless   on the chair   probably
quickly   seldom   until tomorrow

| | |
|---|---|
| adverbs of time | last year |
| frequency adverbs | |
| adverbs of certainty | |
| adverbs of manner | |
| adverbs of place | |
| connecting adverbs | |

**2 Are the adverbs in bold in the right position? Put a tick (✔) by any you think are right and correct the others.**

0 **Definitely** I will help you with your homework tonight. ..........
1 I had never been to the cinema **before the age of 14**. ..........
2 She enjoys **from time to time** going to the beach. ..........
3 **Probably** it won't take you long to get used to it. ..........
4 James ran away when he saw the spider **immediately**. ..........
5 We got dressed **quickly** and went outside. ..........
6 That's a good computer. It's a bit **however** expensive. ..........

**3 Write the words in order to make sentences.**

0 night / we / to a / rock concert / last / went
  ....We went to a rock concert last night.........
1 often / drink / I / coffee / don't
  ....................................................
2 probably / this film / won't / the kids / enjoy
  ....................................................
3 plays / beautifully / she / the piano
  ....................................................
4 finish / next week / I'll / my project
  ....................................................

Unit 6

## LISTENING

**1** Read the five questions in exercise 2 and match each one to what it is focusing on.

a speaker's opinion question .......
b agreement between speakers question .......
c speaker's purpose question .......
d situation question .......
e a specific piece of information question .......

> **EXAM TIPS**
>
> **Listening Part 1**
> - Read the questions carefully before you listen and underline the main ideas in them.
> - Identify any functions the questions may be focusing on, for example the speaker's purpose, agreement between the speakers.
> - Listen to the whole extract before you choose your answer.

**2** You will hear people talking in five different situations. Read the questions, and underline the main ideas that might help you get the correct answers.

1 You hear a teenager leaving a voicemail message. Why is she calling?
  A to apologise for missing an appointment
  B to report on an event
  C to arrange a meeting

2 You hear a boy talking to a friend about something that happened to him. What was he doing at the time?
  A crossing the street
  B riding a bike
  C driving a car

3 You hear two people talking about a school sports day. What did the woman think of it?
  A There weren't enough volunteers.
  B She thought nobody enjoyed it.
  C It achieved its intended goal.

4 You overhear two friends in a shop talking about some trainers. The friends agree that the trainers are
  A too expensive.
  B a nice colour.
  C very comfortable.

5 You overhear two friends talking about comedy. How did the boy first find out about the new DVD?
  A A friend mentioned it to him.
  B It was featured in a magazine.
  C He saw an extract online.

**3** ▶4 Listen to the five situations. For questions 1–5, choose the best answer (A, B or C).

**4** ▶4 Listen again and check your answers.

### Word profile *thing*

Complete the sentences with the phrases below.

| a good thing | a single thing | among other things | no such thing |
| the main thing | the thing is | the whole thing | |

1 It's ..................................... you remembered to charge your phone before you left the house!
2 I think it's time for you to forget about ..................................... and get on with the rest of your life.
3 I'd like to come out this evening, but ..................................... , I've got a big exam tomorrow.
4 Well, the children enjoyed themselves, and that's ..................................... .
5 Do you know what? I can't remember ..................................... about last year's holiday! It must have been really boring!
6 There's plenty to do on the campsite – swimming, tennis and a games room ..................................... .
7 I tried to tell her there was ..................................... as monsters, but she was still scared of entering the old house.

Strong emotions 27

# 7 Telling stories

## VOCABULARY  Verbs of movement; sounds

**1** Find 11 verbs of movement and 5 more verbs describing sounds people make in the word square (→ ↓ ↘ ↗). Then match 12 of them with the definitions.

1. move the top part of your body in a particular direction ..........................
2. knock or touch something gently ..........................
3. hurry or move quickly somewhere ..........................
4. go down into a position where both knees are on the ground ..........................
5. hit someone with the flat, inside part of your hand ..........................
6. move smoothly backwards and forwards ..........................
7. walk slowly in a relaxed way ..........................
8. speak too quietly and not clearly enough for someone to understand you ..........................
9. make a sound by breathing air out through a small hole made with your lips ..........................
10. breathe out slowly and noisily, often because you are annoyed or unhappy ..........................
11. speak extremely quietly so that other people cannot hear ..........................
12. shout very loudly ..........................

| W | H | I | S | P | E | R | U | P | H | E | S |
|---|---|---|---|---|---|---|---|---|---|---|---|
| V | U | T | W | I | J | M | X | N | C | B | H |
| J | T | K | A | G | G | P | M | N | K | U | A |
| E | W | U | N | P | Z | H | U | R | N | R | K |
| T | H | X | D | T | M | O | X | L | R | S | E |
| G | I | Y | E | U | B | F | R | E | Z | T | K |
| S | S | E | R | Q | S | V | T | A | K | F | R |
| W | T | L | Z | P | P | T | E | N | N | Q | U |
| I | L | L | M | M | U | M | B | L | E | D | S |
| N | E | O | S | M | N | O | P | R | E | P | H |
| G | Y | S | Q | P | D | O | X | M | L | P | R |
| S | L | A | P | X | L | C | H | A | R | G | E |

**2** Choose the correct words.

I was sitting at my desk in the history lesson yesterday when the boy behind me ¹ *burst / leant* forward and ² *tapped / bounced* me on the shoulder. 'Can you hear that noise?' he ³ *charged / whispered*? 'No, I can't hear anything,' I ⁴ *muttered / whistled* in reply, and tried to get back to my maths problems. But then, I did hear something, outside in the corridor. Someone was ⁵ *mumbling / whistling* a tune, and it was getting louder. Suddenly the classroom door ⁶ *swung / slapped* open and a man with a pot of paint in each hand ⁷ *knelt / burst* into the room. 'Is this the dining hall?' he asked, obviously in a hurry. Our teacher, who was in a bad mood anyway, ⁸ *yelled / sighed*. 'Does it look like the dining hall?' she asked. 'No, no, I suppose not,' ⁹ *mumbled / bounced* the man – and he turned around and ¹⁰ *slapped / rushed* out of the door. Everyone was ¹¹ *muttering / shaking* with laughter. 'Silence!' our teacher ¹² *yelled / whistled*. 'Get back to work. You can join him in the dining hall in ten minutes.'

## READING

### EXAM TIPS

**Reading and Use of English Part 7**
- Read the questions and texts quickly to get the general meaning.
- Be careful when you find the same words from a question used in a text – think about the meaning and whether it matches the question.
- If you can't decide between two texts, underline the relevant words in both and return to the question later.

**1** ● You are going to read an article about four young novelists. For questions 1–10, choose from the writers A–D. The writers may be chosen more than once.

Which writer...

| | |
|---|---|
| got help from a school employee? | 1 |
| does not expect her next novel to be as successful as the last? | 2 |
| intends to produce a different type of novel next? | 3 |
| asked for feedback from others during the writing process? | 4 |
| was good at something other than writing? | 5 |
| was working on several stories when her first novel was finished? | 6 |
| wore a costume to advertise her book? | 7 |
| produced a novel in order to test herself? | 8 |
| felt a lot of pressure to succeed? | 9 |
| was surprised by her success? | 10 |

**A** Christine Paul

Currently aged 18, Christine Paul was brought up in Australia. Maths was her strongest school subject from an early age, which is why her mother was surprised when, at the age of 12, Christine announced that she wanted to be a novelist. 'I knew I could do it,' she says. 'I never doubted myself.' Her first novel, a historical fantasy called *Elinwood*, was finished when she was just 15, and was published that year by her parents' publishing company. 'My family were a great help, but didn't interfere with my writing,' she says. To promote the novel, Christine toured over a hundred schools and libraries talking about her work, all the time dressed in the clothes of her leading character. She got valuable feedback about her customers from these events and has published three more novels for the same age group since then. However, she now plans to have a go at science fiction. 'We'll wait and see how that turns out,' she says.

**B** Amelia Benson

Amelia Benson wrote her first novel at the age of 13. At that time she said she had over a dozen tales at various stages of completion. Her big break came when her English teacher found out about her work, and contacted a literary agent on her behalf. The novel was published on her fourteenth birthday and, it turns out, was the first in a long series. 'I didn't know at the time whether the first novel would lead on to anything else, but that's how it worked out, luckily,' she says. Now living in London, Amelia isn't planning to give up on the series any time soon, even though she has turned her hand to costume dramas for TV.

**C** Flavia Bujor

After a few years of starting stories that never got finished, Flavia Bujor decided it was time she completed something. So, at the age of 12, she decided to write a novel. 'Writing has been a passion of mine since I was very young,' says Flavia. To be published was like a dream come true for her, something she hadn't thought possible. She wrote the novel, *The Prophecy of the Stones*, primarily to see if she could. She would write a chapter and pass it on to family and school friends to see if they liked it. She's already at work on her second novel, and hopes to improve her style in that. 'The first one was just a beginning,' she says.

**D** Saira Hilton

'In many ways I was a victim of my own early success,' says Saira, whose first novel, *The Outriders*, was published when she was just 16, much to the amazement of her teachers and friends. 'When people praise you as "The Voice of Youth" it can be a difficult thing to live up to.' *The Outriders* was one of the most advertised and bestselling novels of the year, but in spite of having a three-book contract with her publisher, Saira didn't write another word for the next four years. Eventually, with the encouragement of friends at college, she started again. 'I've nearly finished a follow-up to *The Outriders*,' she says. 'I'd be surprised if it does as well, but I'm determined to get it finished. I feel I owe it to myself.'

**2** Read the questions again. Underline the parts of the article which gave you the answers.

**3** Find words in the texts which mean the following.

1. try to get involved in something, in an annoying way (A) ..............................
2. person whose job it is to deal with business for another person (B) ..............................
3. strong love or attraction (C) ..............................
4. be as good as people hope or expect (D) ..............................

### Word profile *patience*

**Complete the sentences with the most appropriate form of *patience/patient*.**

1. Please try not to be ............................ with your younger brother and sister. They're trying their hardest.
2. We waited calmly and ............................ for thirty minutes outside the theatre, then we asked for our money back.
3. The singer thanked us for our ............................ when the band finally came on the stage.
4. You have to be very ............................ to be a primary school teacher.
5. Dinner will be ready in a minute. Stop tapping the table so ............................ .
6. I'd been trying to get through to the shop on the phone all morning, and my ............................ was growing.

Telling stories 29

## GRAMMAR Narrative tenses

**1** Match the beginnings and ends of the sentences.

1. She was walking through the woods
2. By the time we got to the stadium,
3. His hair was wet because
4. I took off my coat
5. The burglar was able to get in easily because
6. We had been travelling for hours
7. As soon as she had spoken,
8. By the time we arrived at the party,

a. the match had already started.
b. when she heard a scream.
c. she regretted it.
d. we hadn't locked the back door.
e. most of our friends had already left.
f. and sat down on the sofa.
g. before we decided to stop and rest.
h. he had been swimming in the river.

1 ...... 2 ...... 3 ...... 4 ......
5 ...... 6 ...... 7 ...... 8 ......

**2** Write the verbs in brackets in the past simple, past perfect simple or past perfect continuous.

1. By the time our meal arrived we ............................ (wait) for an hour and a half.
2. My parents ............................ (not believe) me when I told them I ............................ (pass) every one of my exams.
3. She ............................ (put on) her raincoat, ............................ (pick up) her umbrella, and ............................ (leave) the house.
4. They ............................ (train) all morning in the gym, which is why they ............................ (be) exhausted.
5. I ............................ (only sit) down for a couple of minutes when my brother ............................ (come) in and ............................ (ask) me to help him fix his bike.
6. We ............................ (run) for just over an hour when the thunderstorm ............................ (begin).
7. Everyone ............................ (already start) eating by the time we ............................ (get) home.
8. Even though we ............................ (never meet), I ............................ (recognise) him from his Facebook page.
9. Luisa ............................ (write) short stories since she ............................ (be) a child, and then her favourite magazine ............................ (offer) to publish one of them.
10. Before I ............................ (have) the opportunity to book tickets for the concert, they ............................ (all sell) out.

**3** Write one sentence from the notes, using the correct tenses.

0. when / we / arrive at cinema / 7.40 / film / start
   ...When we arrived at the cinema at 7.40, the film had started.

1. the teacher / talk / fire alarm / ring
   ....................................................................
   ....................................................................

2. Karen / learn Spanish / two years / go to live in Argentina
   ....................................................................
   ....................................................................

3. I leave home / run for the bus / and arrive at school / on time
   ....................................................................
   ....................................................................

4. we get home / Mum finish preparing dinner
   ....................................................................
   ....................................................................

**4** 👁 Choose the correct sentence in each pair.

1. a I received your letter this morning.
   b I had received your letter this morning.
2. a He saw a woman he never met before.
   b He saw a woman he had never met before.
3. a I enjoyed it a lot and would do it again.
   b I had enjoyed it a lot and would do it again.
4. a It was the first time I went to the cinema.
   b It was the first time I had been to the cinema.

## VOCABULARY Time phrases

**1** Make five time phrases then match them with their definitions.

1. for some        no time
2. before          long
3. the week        on end
4. for weeks       before last
5. in              time

a. quite soon
b. very quickly
c. two weeks ago
d. for several weeks
e. for a long period

**2** Choose the correct words.

1. Tim had no trouble settling in to his new school – he got used to it *for some time / in no time*.
2. I went to bed at 11 o'clock and *before long / for days on end* was fast asleep.
3. She had wanted to meet her pen friend *for some time / in no time* and was pleased to get the chance.
4. They finished all their exams *the week before last / for weeks on end*.
5. We waited for the weather to improve *before long / for days on end* but it never did.

## WRITING  A story

See Prepare to write box, Student's Book page 45.

**1** Look at the exam task and make notes below for a possible story.

> You have seen this notice on an English-language website.
>
> > We are looking for stories for our new English-language magazine for young people. Your story must begin with this sentence:
> > *When school finished, I checked my phone and saw the text.*
> > Your story must include:
> > an arrangement
> > a gift
>
> Write your **story**.

What did the message say? ............................................

Who had written it? ............................................

What happened next? ............................................

How did you feel? ............................................

**2** Read the story, ignoring the gaps. Is it similar to your notes? Does it contain all the parts of the question?

> When school finished, I checked my phone and saw the text: It said 'Please meet me outside the library at four. Don't be late!'
>
> The text was from Jim, a classmate from my old school. We ¹............................ (never be) very close friends. In fact, I didn't really like him. Once, I ²............................ (lose) a tennis racket at school, and I always thought that Jim had taken it.
>
> So why did he want to see me now? We ³............................ (not speak) to each other for three years! I was curious, so I ⁴............................ (get) my coat and ⁵............................ (leave) home. The sun ⁶............................ (shine) and I needed to do some shopping anyway. When I got to the library, Jim ⁷............................ (wait) for me. He was the first to speak. 'I want to apologise to you.' 'What for?' I asked. 'I accidentally ⁸............................ (take) your tennis racket at your last school. But I never gave it back and then you left the school. Anyway, here's a new one – I hope you like it.'
>
> It was a much better racket than my old one. I thanked him and went home, surprised and happy. What a strange afternoon!

## EXAM TIPS

**Writing Part 2 (a story)**
- Read the first sentence and think about the situation before you start writing.
- Plan the events in your story, making sure there is a link to the first sentence.
- Be careful to use the correct pronouns and tenses.
- Check your story has a beginning, a middle and an end.

**3** Rewrite your notes from exercise 1 so they are about the story.

What did the message say? (paragraph 1)
...meet at library at four...

Who had written it? (paragraph 2)
............................................

What happened next? (paragraph 3)
............................................

How did you feel? (paragraph 4)
............................................

**4** Now write the verbs in brackets in the story in the correct form.

**5** Underline linkers and expressions of time.

**6** 🔴 Write your own story.

Use the headings in exercises 1 and 3 to plan your story.
Think about the pronouns and tenses you will need to use.
Use linkers to connect the events in your story.
Write 140–190 words.

# 8 A great place to live

## VOCABULARY  Community

**1** Complete the crossword below, using these clues.

**Across**
1. in the central part of a city
3. friendly to visitors
5. of an area with only houses and flats, not offices or factories
6. far away from anywhere
7. seeing or communicating with each other a lot
8. belonging to or relating to a city

**Down**
1. connected with industry and factories
2. comfortable and informal, not tense
4. containing people from many different cultures
6. connected with the countryside

(Crossword: 1 across = INNERCITY)

**2** Find the odd word out.
1. inner city   rural   urban
2. industrial   close   welcoming
3. diverse   urban   inner city
4. residential   remote   industrial

**3** Complete the sentences with words from exercise 1.

1. You won't find many offices or factories here. This is a ............................ area.
2. I wouldn't like to live in a really ............................ place; I like having cafés and shops nearby.
3. London is a very ............................ city, where people from all over the world live and work.
4. Everyone we met seemed really pleased to see us – San Francisco is such a ............................ place.
5. The trouble with living in an ............................ area is that the factories can be quite noisy and polluting.
6. I'd prefer to live somewhere with a ............................ atmosphere, rather than a busy ............................-city area.
7. They are a very ............................ family that do everything together.
8. My aunt and uncle decided to leave ............................ life and the city behind, and they found a lovely village in a ............................ area, surrounded by forests and mountains.

## READING

**1** Look at the photos. Where do you think this city is?

**2** Look through the article quickly and check your answer to exercise 1.

**3** Read the article carefully. The first and last paragraphs are in the correct place, but the others are all in the wrong order. Put them in the correct order, using the underlined links to help you.

1  A   2 ......   3 ......
4 ......   5 ......   6  F

**4** Answer the questions about the article.

1. What do the designers of Masdar hope to achieve?
   ..............................................................
2. What is most energy used for in Abu Dhabi?
   ..............................................................
3. Where did the designers get inspiration from when thinking of ways to cool the city?
   ..............................................................
4. Why were some ideas dropped?
   ..............................................................
5. What are the two main forms of transport in Masdar?
   ..............................................................

# City of the Desert

**A** Imagine that, instead of fighting traffic behind a steering wheel or being squashed with strangers in a hot bus, your morning journey to work or school started in a silent self-driving electric car, powered by the sun, moving through underground tunnels at a comfortable 20 kph. Your petrol cost? Zero. Bus fare? Zero. Journey stress? None at all. In our current oil-dependent world, this might seem impossible, but in a remote part of the Arabian Desert it is becoming a reality.

**B** Energy use in neighbouring Abu Dhabi is extremely high, primarily to satisfy the air-cooling demands created by a growing city located in a roasting desert. Over a period of six years, Abu Dhabi's energy bills increased by more than 400%! That is not something which the designers of Masdar wish to copy.

**C** In the heart of the oil-rich United Arab Emirates, just 30 kilometres east of the capital city of Abu Dhabi, architects and government officials are constructing a carbon-neutral city with the hope that the design will help lead the world towards a greener future. By 2025 it is estimated that Masdar will be a busy city of 90,000 – with everyone living off renewable energy while producing almost no waste or pollution. But how can a city in the middle of a desert operate carbon free? Even with established clean energy sources such as solar and wind power to run the eco-city, the city's architects needed to find a way to limit energy use in a place where weather conditions can be severe. From May to July there is virtually no rain, and average high temperatures in July and August are about 42 degrees.

**D** Some ambitious designs that arose out of the research into the past, like plans to build the city on a seven-metre-high base to increase air flow through the city streets, were dropped due to financial issues, but others remained. One of the most interesting of these is Masdar City's 'wind-tower', a nearly 45-metre-high version of an ancient Middle Eastern design that pulls cool breezes from higher areas down the tower and throws them out into the city streets. Narrow streets and angled buildings were used to increase shade and reduce temperatures from direct sun. In all, the architects estimated they could make Masdar feel 20 degrees cooler, resulting in lower use of air-conditioning.

**E** To avoid Abu Dhabi's troubles, Masdar City's architects sought out a surprising source of inspiration: the past. The architects studied ancient civilisations to come up with a solution to the cooling problem, because if they can solve the cooling problem, they are a long way towards solving the whole energy problem.

**F** In addition to energy-reducing construction, transportation in and around Masdar is designed to reduce the use of petrol. City streets are completely car free – all vehicles must be left in a garage outside of the city's massive wall. Instead a fleet of electric cars is used, alongside an electric rail system. The city is not yet perfect, but if the government and city planners can iron out solutions to transportation and energy production in the face of economic insecurity, and Masdar City continues to build on its current successes, this desert oasis could offer a glimpse into an entirely green future.

**5 Find words in the text which mean the following.**

1. building (C) ..............................
2. guessed (C) ..............................
3. control the amount of something (C) ..............................
4. looked for (E) ..............................
5. very large (F) ..............................

### Word profile *make*

**Rewrite the sentences using the correct form of *make* and the word in brackets.**

0. I couldn't understand what his essay meant. (no)
   His essay *made no sense* to me.
1. The situation would improve if you gave me some money. (difference).
   It would .......................................... if you gave me some money.
2. We should enjoy this good weather while it lasts. (most)
   We should .......................................... this good weather.
3. Were those discount vouchers useful to you? (use)
   Did you .......................................... those discount vouchers?
4. They went to the beach soon after they arrived. (way)
   They .......................................... to the beach soon after they arrived.
5. It's a good idea to take the bus to the shopping centre. (sense)
   It .......................................... to take the bus to the shopping centre.

A great place to live

## GRAMMAR  Future (1): Review

**1** Choose the correct answers. Sometimes two are possible.

1. The taxi's here. We ....... leave for the airport.
   a  're about to    b  will    c  may
2. I think you ....... enjoy living in this city.
   a  are    b  will    c  are going to
3. After I ....... to drive, my dad's going to buy me a car.
   a  'll learn    b  'm learning    c  've learnt
4. Have you decided what you ....... study at university yet?
   a  'll    b  're going to    c  are about to
5. They ....... be hungry when they arrive – I don't know if they've eaten.
   a  'll    b  might    c  're going to
6. I'm not tired yet – I think I ....... watch a DVD before I go to bed.
   a  'll    b  could    c  'm about to
7. What time ....... the train leave for London?
   a  is    b  will    c  does
8. I'm not sure, but I ....... see Rachel in town this afternoon.
   a  might    b  will    c  'm going to

**2** Complete the sentences. Use the best future form of the verbs.

| answer | depart | finish | get | jump | snow | ~~start~~ |

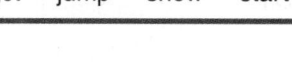

0 They *are about to start* running.

1 It .......................... tomorrow.

2 Don't worry, I .......................... it.

3 I'll meet you when I .......................... this.

4 He .......................... off the cliff.

5 She .......................... a taxi, or she .......................... a train.

6 The plane to Rio .......................... at 7.30.

**3** 👁 Correct the mistakes in these sentences or put a tick (✔) by any you think are correct.

1. We will pick you up from the airport when you'll arrive. ..............
2. I am sure you find lots of interesting things to do during your visit. ..............
3. I hope my suggestion will be useful to you. ..............
4. It's very nice that you will came to London. ..............
5. We will discuss it when you will come home. ..............
6. I'm going to travel by plane, so I'll book the tickets soon. ..............

## VOCABULARY  as if / as though

Write sentences to complete the conversations. Use the prompts in brackets and *as though / as if*.

0 **A:** Oh no! Look at that dog!
  **B:** (look / attack us!)
  *It looks as though it's going to attack us!*

1 **A:** Tony's behaving strangely, isn't he?
  **B:** (yes / act / win the lottery)
  ..............

2 **A:** Why are you phoning a taxi?
  **B:** (look / the bus / late)
  ..............

3 **A:** You don't look very well.
  **B:** (feel / not sleep for days)
  ..............

4 **A:** How did Jane sound when she phoned you last night?
  **B:** (sound / not happy about something)
  ..............

5 **A:** How was your first day back at college?
  **B:** (feel / never be away)
  ..............

6 **A:** Do you know that girl over there?
  **B:** (no / but / act / know us)
  ..............

## LISTENING

### EXAM TIPS

**Listening Part 2**
- Read the notes first and decide what type of information is needed in each gap – usually a noun or noun phrase.
- You will hear the actual words you need to write in the recording.
- Check your answers when you listen the second time. Be careful to spell everything correctly.

**1** Look at each gap in the notes below. Guess what kind of information from the list below is needed to fill the gap. (Two items from the list are used twice.)

|                              | Gap(s)        |
|------------------------------|---------------|
| a game or sport              | ...........   |
| a geographical feature, place| ...........   ........... |
| a task                       | ...........   |
| an ability                   | ...........   |
| a qualification              | ...........   |
| a type of media              | ...........   |
| a food item                  | ...........   |
| a subject / topic            | ...........   ........... |

**2** Read the notes below quickly. What is Sara's talk about?

...................................................................................................

**3** ▶5 You will hear a talk by a girl called Sara Richardson who was a volunteer on a conservation project. For questions 1–10, complete the sentences with a word or short phrase.

### Conservation project

It was Sara's interest in **(1)** ........................... which made her want to work on the conservation project.
Sara says that the project gave her useful information which helped with her **(2)** ........................... .
Sara slept in the camp that was near **(3)** ........................... .
Sara did not enjoy **(4)** ........................... when she was on 'camp duty'.
Sara missed eating her **(5)** ........................... , which wasn't available.
Sara learnt the skill of **(6)** ........................... , which is useful to her in her work at the moment.
Sara's camera took particularly good photographs of **(7)** ........................... .
During quiet periods, the volunteers would play **(8)** ........................... and chess.
Sara mentions a **(9)** ........................... where people are allowed to feed the animals.
Sara has produced a **(10)** ........................... about her time on the conservation project.

A great place to live

# 9 Being positive

## VOCABULARY Collocations

**1** Match the two halves of the collocations.

| | | | |
|---|---|---|---|
| 1 | achieve | a | the best of |
| 2 | go | b | bright |
| 3 | have | c | every opportunity |
| 4 | have | d | the best in |
| 5 | look | e | the worst in |
| 6 | make | f | your goals |
| 7 | make | g | wrong |
| 8 | make | h | a go |
| 9 | put | i | the most of |
| 10 | see | j | strengths and weaknesses |
| 11 | see | k | a difference |
| 12 | take | l | an end to |

1 ....... 2 ....... 3 ....... 4 .......
5 ....... 6 ....... 7 ....... 8 .......
9 ....... 10 ....... 11 ....... 12 .......

**2** Complete the sentences with the correct form of the collocations from exercise 1.

1 Sally is an optimist. She always thinks the future ............................... .
2 You will only ............................... your ............................... if you work hard.
3 Why do you ............................... to criticise my work? It's very discouraging.
4 The project was a disaster. Everything ............................... .
5 Although the weather was terrible, and the hotel was noisy, we ............................... a bad situation, and had a good holiday.
6 We scored a goal in the last minute, but it didn't ............................... to the final result – we still lost the match.
7 I had never tried skiing before, but I ............................... when I visited friends in Austria, and was quite good at it.
8 He always tries to ............................... people, which is why he is often disappointed when they let him down.
9 As a chess player, Mark ............................... – he's good at attacking, but not so good at defending.
10 Let's try to ............................... our last two days off before school starts again.
11 She broke her leg last year, which ............................... her tennis career.
12 I think someone has hurt Sarah badly – she always ............................... people.

## READING

**1** Read the article quickly. Would you describe the writer as an optimist or a pessimist?

### EXAM TIPS

**Reading and Use of English Part 5**
- Read the text quickly to get an idea of what it's about.
- Read through the questions and ABCD options carefully.
- Answer each one in order – remember that they follow the order of information in the text.
- Underline the parts of the text where you find the answer.

**2** The answers to questions 1 and 2 are underlined. Read the questions and choose the answer (A, B, C or D) which you think fits best according to the text.

1 According to the first paragraph, how did the writer feel when he received his mother's texts?
 A They made him very concerned about her.
 B He thought her suggestions were interesting.
 C They convinced him to come home immediately.
 D He realised that she wanted the best for him.
2 The writer finally decided to return to Britain because
 A he had to leave the flat he was living in.
 B he liked the idea of selling mobile phones.
 C he thought it was time to leave Belgium.
 D he wanted to be close to his family.

**3** For questions 3 to 6, choose the answer (A, B, C or D) which you think fits best according to the text.

3 How did the writer feel about his training?
 A surprised that it was so brief
 B annoyed by the attitude of the instructor
 C worried by the amount of reading involved
 D pleased that it was so successful
4 The writer told the taxi driver to 'just keep driving' because
 A he had forgotten his parents' address.
 B he wanted to practise his sales technique.
 C he thought the taxi driver was lost.
 D he needed time to think about his future.
5 What does the writer mean by 'it was paying dividends' in paragraph 6?
 A providing financial reward
 B creating opportunities to meet people
 C helping others with their lives
 D bringing good luck
6 What is the writer's attitude to his work?
 A He regards it as necessary to make money.
 B He doesn't think he'll be doing it in a few years.
 C He finds it hard to keep up with the technology.
 D He sees it as an important part of his life.

# MY LIFE IN SALES

A year ago I'd left school, I was 18, and I was living in Brussels. My mother was texting me almost every day about the awful jobs market in Britain, trying to persuade me to come home and start a university course to give me better job opportunities. However, her ideas were all really dull: train as an accountant, study law, become a teacher. I was living with a group of friends in a flat in the centre of town, having fun. I knew Mum's suggestions were well-intentioned and the result of nights spent worrying about me. However, they didn't exactly grab my attention.

Then yet another text appeared: how about selling mobile phones. Surely this was a bit desperate! But, thinking about it, I had no desire to spend the rest of my life in Belgium, fun as it was, so I informed my landlord and flatmates that I'd be leaving in two weeks and arranged an interview with a new company called Mobiles-r-Us, based in central Birmingham, not far from where my parents lived.

Their shop was located in a shopping mall right in the middle of the city, and I found it easily. The interview went well and I got the job. I had expected to be given some intensive training for this sales role, but the only guidance I received followed immediately after the interview, lasting all of five minutes. Afterwards, the manager opened his drawer and took out a dozen year-long contracts and a sales script. Holding them out to me, he said, 'Read the script and learn it, then come back tomorrow, stand outside the shop, and start selling those phones.' Astonished that I was expected to start work already, I muttered something about finding customers. He took me to the entrance of the shop and we watched the crowds of people walking past for a while. 'Customers,' he said.

Eager to get home and learn the script, and determined to start earning my living as soon as possible, I stopped a taxi outside the shopping mall. I told the driver the name of the suburb where my parents lived and started reading the script to myself. When we got close, he asked for the actual address, but as I was only halfway through the script, I said 'Just keep driving for now,' and I began to read it aloud. 'Have you seen the amazing new mobile phone contract from Mobiles-r-Us?' I asked. After practising my script for ten more minutes, I said to the driver, 'So, are you ready to upgrade your phone and change to Mobiles-r-Us for a year, with a free month's trial?' 'That sounds like a good deal,' said the taxi driver and he signed on the dotted line.

It's hard to express the feeling I experienced at that moment. I imagine a footballer has similar emotions when he scores the winning goal in an important match. All I can say is that I felt that I had arrived. That I had found the thing I was good at and that doing it better and better was what I wanted to do from then on.

I didn't know the average salesman sells only 15 mobile phone contracts a month, and I soon broke all the records by selling several times that, to everyone from lawyers to cleaners. I was making a small fortune in bonuses! I had always been good at getting people to do what I wanted, ever since I was a boy, and at last it was paying dividends. Soon I was able to move out of my parents' home, and into my own flat.

I'm still selling mobile phones a year later. Will I still be doing it in ten years' time? I honestly can't say. It's quite possible that I will get tired of selling mobile phones – even though the technology is moving so fast and features change every few months. It's essential to keep moving if you want to get on. But there is one thing I am sure of: I'll never get tired of the thrill I get when I make a successful sale. That feeling will stay with me until the day I finally retire – why would I ever stop doing something I love doing?

**4** Now underline the parts of the text which gave you the answers in exercise 3.

## Word profile *hold*

Match the beginnings and ends of the sentences.

1 **Hold on**! That's not fair – .......
2 Yes, I'll ask John to help us .......
3 He's great at swimming underwater .......
4 I'm not sure if Mark's at home; .......
5 Try to **get hold of** their latest CD – .......
6 He was winning for the first 200 metres .......
7 Do you know who **holds** the world record .......

a because he can **hold** his breath for ages.
b it's fantastic.
c but he couldn't **hold on** to the lead.
d **hold on**, I'll phone him and see.
e that's not what I said!
f if I can **get hold of** him.
g for the 100 m sprint?

Being positive 37

## GRAMMAR Future (2): Continuous and perfect

**1 Choose the correct future form.**

1 If you keep spending like that, *you'll be spending / you'll have spent* all of your money before we go.
2 Please don't phone me before 7.00 because *I'll have slept / I'll be sleeping* at that time.
3 By the end of this year, the twins *will be going / will have been going* to this school for three years.
4 I'll be free at 5.00 because *I'll be finishing / I'll have finished* all my homework by then.
5 We can't call on Pippa yet; *she'll be working / she'll have been working* on her music project.
6 My grandfather *will be living / will have been living* in the same house for fifty years in December.
7 When we finally arrive at our destination, *we'll have travelled / we'll have been travelling* 2,456 km!
8 If you want to talk to Simon, *he'll be studying / he'll have studied* in the library after lunch.

**2 Complete the sentences with one of the verbs below in the future perfect simple or continuous.**

| arrive | be | build | cook |
| finish | read | wait | write |

1 By Friday afternoon, I ................................. this essay for four days!
2 Don't come round at five o'clock on Thursday – I ................................. (not) football practice by then.
3 They're having an anniversary party next week. They ................................. married for five years.
4 Do you think you ................................. this book by the end of the month?
5 By next summer, they ................................. this bridge for five years – and it's still not finished!
6 I hope Dad ................................. dinner for us when we get home. I'm starving!
7 I'm going home in five minutes. I ................................. for them to arrive for exactly an hour by then.
8 By this time tomorrow, we ................................. at the holiday resort.

**3 ⊙ Correct the mistakes in these sentences or put a tick (✔) by any you think are correct.**

1 I have finished my examinations in a couple of days and then I'm going to a small island.
.................................
2 When the concert will have finished you can interview the conductor of the orchestra.
.................................
3 I will be continuing for four days and finish on Saturday. .................................
4 When I arrive, I'll be wearing jeans and a green T-shirt. .................................

## VOCABULARY Adjective and noun suffixes

**1 Make these words into nouns or adjectives, and write them in the correct column below. Be careful to make any spelling changes necessary.**

| Nouns: | compete  encourage  enjoy  friend  major  personal  relation  responsible  satisfy |

| Adjectives: | act  benefit  effect  emotion  practice  remark  value |

| Nouns | |
|---|---|
| -ity | |
| -ment | |
| -ship | |
| -tion | |

| Adjectives | |
|---|---|
| -able | |
| -al | |
| -ive | |

**2 Complete the sentences with a noun or adjective from exercise 1.**

1 I always feel very ........................... when I watch romantic films.
2 Danny will do well, but he needs a lot of ........................... because he isn't very confident.
3 Who won first prize in the fancy dress ...........................?
4 My bicycle was stolen but I'm not too sad because it wasn't very ........................... .
5 She denied all ........................... for the mistakes that were made.
6 The ........................... of students are in favour of having longer summer holidays.
7 We tried to fix the hole with some newspaper, but it wasn't ........................... at all.
8 It spoils my ........................... of a film when there are noisy people in the cinema.
9 We had such a big argument that it threatened our ........................... at one point, but we soon forgave each other and are now closer than ever.
10 My lifestyle is quite ...........................; I swim twice a week, and I usually ride my bike to school.

Unit 9

# WRITING  An article (2)

See Prepare to write box, Student's Book page 35.

## EXAM TIPS

**Writing Part 2 (an article)**
- Make notes in answer to each point or question in the task.
- Organise your notes into a plan before writing.
- Introduce each paragraph with a topic sentence.

**1** Look at the questions in the exam task. Make notes of your answers.

.................................................................................
.................................................................................
.................................................................................
.................................................................................
.................................................................................

> You have seen this announcement on an English-language website for students.
>
> **My perfect school**
> If you could choose any school or university to go to, where would it be located? What kind of things would you be able to do there? What facilities would it have?
> The best articles will be published here on our website.
>
> Write your **article**.

**2** Read the article below, ignoring the gaps. Has the writer answered all the questions? Are any of the answers similar to yours?

**3** In this article the topic sentences have been removed, i.e. the first sentence of each paragraph, which introduces the topic. What might each one say?

A  *It might describe the type of location.*
B  .................................................................................
C  .................................................................................
D  .................................................................................

**4** These are the topic sentences from the article. Match them to the paragraphs.

1 It would also have incredible sports facilities.   .......
2 My perfect university would be located in the middle of a cool city.   .......
3 There would be luxury accommodation for those students who don't live nearby.   .......
4 Every classroom would be equipped with the most awesome computer technology.   .......

**5** Look at the structure of the essay. Which paragraph deals with these topics?

1 living   .......
2 leisure   .......
3 location   .......
4 learning   .......

**6** Articles often use informal language, and address the reader directly. Read the article (and the topic sentences) again.

1 Find four informal adjectives (one in each paragraph 1–4):
........................  ........................  ........................
........................

2 Underline two sentences where the reader is addressed directly.

**7** 🔵 Use your notes from exercise 2 and the paragraph headings in Exercise 5 to organise your article. Then write it using 140–190 words.

---

### My perfect university

A  ....... I'd like it to be somewhere like New York or Rome. It would be near shops, cinemas, museums and theatres. But it would be such a big university that it would have shops and cinemas of its own, so you wouldn't have to leave it very often.

B  ....... They should all be free for the students to use when they want, of course. There would also be a huge park, with trees and a lake, where students can walk alone in a peaceful atmosphere. Wouldn't that be great?

C  ....... Also, each room should have free wi-fi for students who want to bring in their own computers. Even better, class sizes would be small, with fifteen students at most, so the teacher can give full attention to each individual.

D  ....... Every student would have a large bedroom and a study. And, on top of all that, the university restaurant would be really fantastic, and serve the most delicious food!

I'd definitely go there! Would you?

# 10 Surprise!

## VOCABULARY  Phrases with *in, out of, at, by*

**1** Complete the sentences with *in, out of, at* or *by*.

1 I didn't mean to delete the email – I did it ............ accident.
2 We met ............ secret to plan Marta's surprise party.
3 It was completely ............ character for David to lose his temper like that.
4 Please let me know ............ advance if you can't come to dinner.
5 Sixteen people ............ all turned up to watch our first performance.
6 I'll answer any questions you have ............ detail during the class tomorrow.
7 She found out completely ............ chance that her friend had moved house.
8 The car driver admitted he was ............ fault for the accident.
9 Don't give your details on social media websites – they're ............ risk of being misused.
10 The boy on the skateboard appeared ............ nowhere and ran straight into me!

**2** Match the phrases with the definitions.

1 in touch        a no longer a popular style
2 at your best    b having shared characteristics
3 out of fashion  c being in top condition
4 by heart        d having contact with
5 in common       e so that you remember all of something
6 in public       f in a place where everyone can see

1 ......  2 ......  3 ......  4 ......  5 ......  6 ......

**3** Complete the sentences so that they mean the same as the one above. Include a phrase from exercises 1 or 2.

1 All my friends use text messaging to stay in contact.
   All my friends keep .........................................................

2 This message has suddenly appeared on my screen.
   This message has appeared ..................................

3 I have a great group of friends. We all like doing the same things.
   I have a great group of friends. We have ..................

4 I'll tell you all about my problem tomorrow.
   I'll tell you about my problem ..................................

5 Rachel and I hadn't seen each other for years but we met at the gym without planning it.
   Rachel and I hadn't seen each other for years but we met ...............................................

**4** Answer the questions about you.

1 What was the last thing you did in secret?
   ...............................................................................
2 Have you ever done anything out of character? What?
   ...............................................................................
3 How far in advance do you make arrangements for the weekend?
   ...............................................................................
4 How many cousins do you have in all?
   ...............................................................................
5 When was the last time you did something by accident?
   ...............................................................................
6 Have you ever been blamed for something when you weren't at fault?
   ...............................................................................

## READING

**1** Look at the definition of *coincidence*. Have you ever experienced a coincidence? What happened?
...............................................................................

> **coincidence (n):** when two very similar things happen at the same time but there is no reason for it

**2** The sections A–F in the article on page 41 are in the wrong order. Read the article and put them in the correct order.

1 ..D..   2 ......   3 ......
4 ......   5 ......   6 ......

**3** Choose the best title for the article.

a Coincidences – magic or maths?
b Great coincidences in history
c No such thing as coincidences

40  Unit 10

**A** Then there is the case of Joseph Figlock, a resident of Detroit USA in the 1930s. He was walking down the street when a baby fell from a high window onto him. The baby survived the fall, and both man and baby were unharmed. This was a stroke of luck on its own, but a year later, the very same baby fell from the very same window onto poor Joseph Figlock as he was once again passing underneath. And once again, they both survived the event.

**B** On July 28th, 1900, the King of Italy, Umberto 1, was having dinner in a restaurant in the city of Monza. He was surprised to discover that the restaurant owner was also called Umberto and that he both looked and spoke almost exactly like him. It was soon revealed that they were born in Turin on the same day, that the restaurant owner had married a woman called Margherita – the name of the queen whom Umberto had married on the same day – and that the restaurant was opened on the day of the King's coronation. Sadly, the restaurant owner was shot dead the next morning. Then, later that same day, King Umberto I was also shot dead.

**C** Considering there are seven billion people on the planet, improbable occurrences are to be expected. Even dreams which appear to predict the future can be explained by the Law of Large Numbers. When seven billion people all dream for two hours per night, some of those dreams are bound to 'come true' the next day. Similarly, someone is sure to meet someone who looks like him/herself and falling babies are likely to land on the same person – very, very rarely.

**D** Coincidences almost never fail to surprise us. An unexpected meeting in an unexpected location, an event that happened at the same time as another event, a dream that appeared to come true the next day – there are many varieties of coincidence. But are they just two chance events, with no special meaning? Or do they have a deeper meaning? Here are a couple of examples for you to consider.

**E** As mathematics professor John Allen Paulos says, 'In reality, the most astonishingly incredible coincidence would be the complete absence of all coincidence.' What? No coincidences at all? Ever? That *would* be a surprise!

**F** So what are we to make of these extraordinary events? One explanation is known as the Law of Large Numbers. This says that with a large enough sample, many strange coincidences are likely to happen. The trouble is, we humans find it very difficult to understand large numbers.

**4** The information in all these sentences except one is incorrect. Tick (✔) the true sentence and correct the others.

1 King Umberto was surprised to find the restaurant owner had been married to the same woman as him. ...........................
2 The restaurant owner died after King Umberto. ...........................
3 Joseph Figlock was injured twice by the same baby. ...........................
4 The Law of Large Numbers says that coincidences are expected to happen. ...........................
5 John Allen Paulos is very surprised that coincidences happen. ...........................

**5** Find words in the article which mean the following.

1 did not die (A) ...........................
2 (of surprising information) told or given (B) ...........................
3 to think about (D) ...........................
4 lack of (E) ...........................

# GRAMMAR  Modals (2): Modals in the past

**1** Choose the correct answer.

1. No wonder Jane is angry with you. You *shouldn't / wouldn't / needn't* have forgotten her birthday!
2. It was an amazing show. You *would have / should have / didn't need to* bought a ticket when you had the chance.
3. We *needn't have taken / shouldn't have taken / didn't need to take* any food to the party because we knew there would be lots there.
4. I'm sorry. I *would / should / wouldn't* have told you that I wasn't coming out tonight.
5. She thought she was going to fail, but she *wouldn't / should / needn't* have worried. She passed easily!
6. I *should / would / needn't* have been so disappointed if we had missed your concert last night.
7. We *needn't / should / wouldn't* have run all the way to the station. The train was an hour late!
8. You *shouldn't have / didn't need to / wouldn't have* been so rude to that man!

**2** Look at the pictures and complete the sentences. Use *should have* or *shouldn't have* and one of the verbs below.

  buy   eat   ~~lock~~   play   remember   study

0. She ...*should have locked*... her bike.
1. He .................................... so much cake. 
2. He .................................... his umbrella. 
3. She .................................... so many things. 
4. She .................................... more. 
5. They .................................... computer games unitl 3.00 a.m. 

**3** Complete the conversations. Use a modal verb + *have* and the verbs in brackets.

1. **A:** You .................................... (ask) Tom before you borrowed his bike. He thought it had been stolen.
   **B:** But maybe he .................................... (let) me borrow it – and I really needed to get to the library before it closed!
   **A:** It doesn't matter. You .................................... (take) it. He was really worried.
   **B:** Well he .................................... (worry). I brought it straight back when I'd finished!

2. **A:** I .................................... (eat) that slice of yesterday's pizza. I feel ill now.
   **B:** You .................................... (tell) me you were hungry. I .................................... (cook) something for you.
   **A:** I thought that I .................................... (ask) you to cook anything because there was a slice of pizza on the table!

3. **A:** Did you go to the last lecture in the history course?
   **B:** No, I .................................... (go) as I'd already done enough to pass the course. I .................................... (be) able to go anyway as I was away last week.
   **A:** It was interesting. I .................................... (attend) it either as I'd passed the course too, but I'm glad I did.

4. **A:** Thank you for the lovely present. You really .................................... (spend) so much money on me. You can't afford it!
   **B:** I know, but you deserve it. I .................................... (get) the summer job in the restaurant without you.
   **A:** That's not true. You .................................... (ask) me for help. They .................................... (employ) you anyway. You were perfect for the job!

**4** 🎧 Correct the mistakes in these sentences or put a tick (✓) by any you think are correct.

1. It had been better to stay in bed.
   ....................................
2. I wondered how it would be without you.
   ....................................
3. It's OK if he really wanted to understand.
   ....................................
4. I shouldn't had done this, because I failed the test.
   ....................................
5. According to the advertisement, the show should have started at 19.30.
   ....................................
6. We had mountain bikes, so we thought that it could be a great idea to visit the forest.
   ....................................

**42**  Unit 10

## VOCABULARY  Extended meanings of words

**1 Match the words with their 'extended meanings'.**

1 boiling    a stood very still
2 flooded    b badly affected
3 froze    c questioned thoroughly or aggressively
4 bright    d very warm
5 grilled    e unclear
6 foggy    f happy and hopeful
7 hit    g arrived in large numbers or amounts
8 angel    h a very good person

1 ......  2 ......  3 ......  4 ......
5 ......  6 ......  7 ......  8 ......

**2 Complete the sentences with a word from exercise 1.**

1 Of course I'll babysit for your little boy – he's an ................................ .
2 My understanding of this is a bit ................................, because the teacher didn't explain it very clearly.
3 The head teacher ................................ the student for half an hour before letting him go.
4 You don't need your coat today – it's ................................ outside!
5 The crowd ................................ into the theatre when the doors opened at 7.00.
6 The loss of his student grant ................................ him very hard.
7 I have a new job and a new flat, so the future is looking ................................ for me at the moment.
8 She ................................ in fear when she saw the large dog running towards her.

## LISTENING

**1 You will hear a man called Rob Mitchell, who works as a party planner, talking about his work. What do you think are the most important things about planning a good party?**

### EXAM TIPS

**Listening Part 4**
- Remember that you have one minute for this part before the recording starts to prepare yourself.
- Read the questions and options carefully to get an idea of what the speakers will be talking about.
- Underline the important words and listen for the ideas they express.

**2 ▶6 Look at question 1 and the underlined key words. Then listen to the first part of the interview and choose the correct answer.**

1 What does Rob say about the job of party planning?
   A It's <u>enjoyable but quite stressful</u>.
   B It makes <u>going to parties more fun</u>.
   C It's <u>not</u> a good job <u>for shy people</u>.

**3 Look at this paragraph from the interview and underline the parts which gave you the answer.**

> Well, I certainly like doing it – but that's not to say it's one big party. It's a business, obviously, and you have to please the client. Just because you're throwing a party doesn't mean it's party time for you. There's a lot of work and a lot of worry involved, and you really can't relax until the last guest has left, and the venue is cleaned up. But if you don't mind working long hours, then yes – it's a fun job, and even better if you enjoy the social aspects.

**4 ▶6 Read questions 2–6. Listen to the interview and for questions 2–6 choose the best answer (A, B or C).**

2 How did Rob get started in party planning?
   A He was encouraged by his parents.
   B A chance meeting led to employment.
   C An events company was looking for an artist.
3 What does Rob say about celebrity clients?
   A They try to pay less money for their parties.
   B They are rather difficult to work with.
   C They are less demanding than other wealthy people.
4 What was the problem with monkeys being involved with one party?
   A They cost too much money.
   B They were a danger to guests.
   C They caused a lot of mess.
5 In Rob's opinion, the essential ingredient for a successful party is
   A the imagination of the planner.
   B the size of the party space.
   C the people who attend.
6 What does Rob enjoy most about his job?
   A having the opportunity to meet celebrities
   B being in an unpredictable situation
   C earning a considerable amount

### Word profile *expect*

**Complete the sentences with the correct form of *expect* or words formed from it.**

1 The main thing about any surprise is that it is ................................ . If it isn't, it isn't a surprise!
2 Don't worry. You're not ................................ to be successful the first time you try.
3 That film didn't really live up to my ................................ , I'm afraid.
4 I ................................ bumped into Tony when I was in the library yesterday.
5 She's ................................ you to buy her a very expensive birthday present this year!
6 Tom's always late. He'll be here soon, I ................................ .

Surprise! 43

# 11 The family unit

## VOCABULARY  Phrasal verbs: relationships

**1** Complete the crossword, using the clues on the right.

**Across**

4 If someone looks … on you, they think they are better than you.
5 When you go … someone, you don't like them any more.
8 A reliable person will not … you down.
9 To '… it off' means that you get on well with somebody straight away.
10 If you … after somebody in your family, it means you have inherited some of their characteristics.

**Down**

1 To '… up to' someone means to admire them.
2 When you … with someone, you end the relationship.
3 If you can … on someone, that means you can rely on them.
6 To '… out with' means that you have an argument.
7 People who … together always support each other.

**2** Use a verb from Box A with a word from Box B to make phrasal verbs. Complete the text with the correct form of the phrasal verb.

Box A: count   fall   go   hit   let   look   look   stick   take

Box B: after   down   down on   off   off   on   out   together   up to

My name's Maria, and I come from a very close family – we always ¹.......................... . My mother is my role model – I really ².......................... her. I think I ³.......................... my mother as she's quite shy and has only two really close friends. I'm quite shy and don't make friends easily either, but when I do become friends with someone, I'm very loyal. You can always ⁴.......................... me to stand by you in your time of need. I will never ⁵.......................... you .......................... ! I don't like people who ⁶.......................... others and think they're better. If you do that, we will probably ⁷.......................... with each other. We might get on with each other at first; maybe we ⁸.......................... it .......................... straight away because we both like the same music or something. But I will ⁹.......................... you very quickly if I hear you talking about somebody else in an unpleasant way!
Please leave a message below if you want to chat.
Maria

## READING

**1** Complete the table with the different forms of the words.

| | noun | verb | adjective | adverb |
|---|---|---|---|---|
| 1 | accident | xxxx | | |
| 2 | .......... | assist | xxxx | xxxx |
| 3 | .......... | xxxx | brave | .......... |
| 4 | belief | .......... | .......... | .......... |
| 5 | .......... | xxxx | confident | .......... |
| 6 | .......... | doubt | .......... | .......... |
| 7 | practice | .......... | .......... | .......... |
| 8 | proof | .......... | xxxx | xxxx |

## 2
**Decide whether a noun, verb, adjective or adverb will fit in each gap in these sentences. Then complete the sentences with a word from exercise 1.**

1 This invention is of no ............................ value.
2 We had to ask for ............................ in completing the project.
3 They ............................ discovered the drug while they were doing research.
4 The police were not able to ............................ that he had done anything illegal.
5 He acted ............................ and managed to save everyone from the fire.
6 It is extremely ............................ that they will be able to do anything about it.
7 Some people lack the ............................ to speak publicly.
8 Some people will ............................ anything they read in the newspapers.

## 3
**Write the opposite of these words by adding un-, im-, in-, mis- or dis-.**

1 polite
2 likely
3 agree
4 correct
5 honest
6 possible
7 happy
8 understand

### EXAM TIPS

**Reading and Use of English Part 3**
- Read the whole text first, to get an idea of what it is about.
- Look carefully at each gap to decide what type of word is needed – a noun, a verb, an adjective or an adverb?
- Make sure that the word you form makes sense in the sentence – does it need to be in the plural or should it have a negative prefix?

## 4
**For questions 1–8, read the text below. Use the word given in capitals at the end of some of the lines to form a word that fits in the gap in the same line. There is an example at the beginning (0).**

Most people think of snakes as solitary, (0) ...aggressive... creatures. The — **AGGRESSION**
idea that they have a caring, family-loving side might seem (1) ............................ , — **LIKELY**
but that is exactly what a new study of rattlesnakes in the USA has revealed.
(2) ............................ have discovered that female rattlesnakes choose to build — **SCIENCE**
their nests close to those of their sisters, even if the animals weren't raised
together. These (3) ............................ , recently published in the journal *Biology* — **FIND**
*Letters*, suggest that it is (4) ............................ for the snakes to stay together in — **BENEFIT**
family groups.
However, this tendency to group together also has some disadvantages, for
example, there is more (5) ............................ for food. Also, predators can return — **COMPETE**
again and again to attack group members. On the other hand, being in a group
improves the snakes' (6) ............................ to defend themselves. — **ABLE**
Although other reptiles have long been known to show sociable
(7) ............................ , this is the first time that the — **BEHAVE**
(8) ............................ has been made about snakes. — **OBSERVE**
With new research being done all the time, the snake's
reputation may eventually be proved wrong.

### EP Word profile *all*

**Choose the correct answer, a, b, or c.**

1 You don't have to start all ........ just because you made one mistake.
   a in all   b over again   c of a sudden
2 I'd like to travel all ........ before I start university.
   a along   b in all   c over the place
3 All ........ , that was a very successful trip.
   a along   b in all   c over again
4 We were very surprised when it started to rain all ........ .
   a of a sudden   b along   c in all
5 I knew all ........ that this course was going to be difficult.
   a in all   b over again   c along
6 About 700 students ........ all signed the petition to get Mr Banks his job back.
   a in   b along   c over

## GRAMMAR  Relative clauses

**1  Cross out the pronouns that can be left out.**

0  The book ~~that~~ I read last week is going to be made into a film.
1  Is that the man who found your laptop?
2  The steak that I ate last night wasn't very good.
3  Are those the children whose teacher is from Brazil?
4  We didn't enjoy the film that we watched last night.
5  This car, which we bought last summer, is very slow.
6  My best friend, who I've known since we were at primary school, is moving to France.

**2  Complete the sentences with *who* or *which*. If the pronoun can be left out, put it in brackets.**

1  My uncle, ........................... writes horror novels, lives in America.
2  We're looking for a house ........................... has four bedrooms.
3  Tell me about the last football match ........................... you played in.
4  My grandmother doesn't trust people ........................... can't cook.
5  Did you ever meet that penfriend ........................... you were writing to?
6  My bike, ........................... I bought with my birthday money, has been stolen.

**3  Match 1–6 to a–f, then join them with *when, where, which, who* or *whose* to make sentences with defining relative clauses. Make any other changes necessary.**

1  A redhead is a person …
2  Moscow is the city …
3  I'll never forget that time …
4  This is the house …
5  There aren't many taxi drivers …
6  There's that boy …

a  It's famous for the Kremlin.
b  We went to the seaside in the rain.
c  His father teaches at my college.
d  My grandfather was born here.
e  Their hair is red.
f  They have never had an accident.

1  *e  A redhead is a person whose hair is red.*
2  ...........................................................................
3  ...........................................................................
4  ...........................................................................
5  ...........................................................................
6  ...........................................................................

**4  Correct the mistakes in these sentences or put a tick (✓) by any you think are correct.**

1  You are lucky because I've got the information who you need about the new art class. ...........
2  You will go to Protagona 7 who has a little supermarket. ...........
3  One morning we went to the beach wich was about 30 minutes from our campsite. ...........
4  Tina had dreamed of winning a ballet contest since she was five years old, that was when she started her lessons. ...........
5  It was a book by Shakespeare, so it is Shakespeare to blame, not me! ...........

## VOCABULARY  Compound adjectives

**1  Complete the text with the words below.**

| balanced | behaved | confident |
| grown | organised | tech |

My best friend's mother is quite strict when it comes to parenting. When the children were young, they were always punished when they were ¹ badly ........................... , and rewarded when they were good. Their lives were very ² well ........................... , with strict times for going to bed and getting up in the mornings. No computers or ³ high-........................... equipment were allowed in their rooms. Their mother was also careful to provide them both with a ⁴ well-........................... diet. It seems to have worked, because now that my friend and his sister are ⁵...........................-up, they are very mature and ⁶ self-........................... young adults.

**2  Combine one word from each column and match them to the definitions.**

| middle- | distance |
| well- | aged |
| last- | term |
| long- | paid |
| short- | built |
| well- | minute |

1  having a large, strong body ...........
2  travelling or communicating between two places that are a long way apart ...........
3  done at the latest possible opportunity ...........
4  in the middle of your life before you are old ...........
5  earning a lot of money ...........
6  lasting a short time, or relating to a short period of time ...........

46  Unit 11

## WRITING  An essay (2)

See Prepare to write box, Student's Book page 57.

**1** Complete the table with the linking words and phrases in bold, according to their function.

1 I enjoy computer games, **whereas** my brother can't stand them.
2 **In my view,** the conditions for economic growth are all in place.
3 Children today have a lot of freedom **compared to/with** children forty years ago.
4 **On balance,** I think it is better to study for a career rather than study for pleasure.
5 The new stadium will force a lot of people to move. **Furthermore**, the city cannot afford it.
6 This is a badly written essay. **Moreover**, it has been copied from the internet!
7 Most people hate the rain. **In contrast**, I love going out when it's really pouring down!
8 **On the one hand**, I think global warming is causing a lot of damage. **On the other hand**, I'm enjoying the weather.
9 **To sum up**, it is a very bad idea to allow children under the age of 12 to work.
10 People in hotter countries spend less on heating. **In addition**, the sun can used for heating water.

| Adding a new point | Furthermore |
|---|---|
| Comparing/contrasting | |
| Concluding | |

**2** Your English teacher has asked you to write an essay. Read the title and add some information for each note.

---

**Write an essay using all the notes and give the reasons for your point of view.**

It is better to be part of a big family than a small family.

**Notes**
Write about:
1 home life – *space, freedom*
2 money
3 ................................................ (your own idea)

---

## EXAM TIPS

**Writing Part 1 (an essay)**
- Use neutral language in the essay (not informal).
- Make sure your essay is quite impersonal – don't use the pronoun *I* too often, though you can give your opinion.
- Learn to use a range of linkers.

**3** Read the essay. Fill in the gaps with linking words and phrases from exercise 1.

*Many people in small families of one or two children imagine that it would be nice to have a bigger family. ¹................................, many people in large families might like to be part of a smaller family group! Is one really better than the other? ²................................, it is often said that large families with four or more children are great fun. Children from large families tend to be more socially confident. ³................................, when the children grow up, they appreciate the life-long friendship and support of their brothers and sisters.*
*⁴................................, it is true that smaller families have a lot more money to spend on themselves! They can go on better holidays, and they can all fit in one car. It is very expensive for a family of, say, nine people to go anywhere. ⁵................................, people in smaller families often have more space and more privacy at home. ⁶................................, there are advantages and disadvantages about both sizes of family. ⁷................................, I think a medium-sized family with two or three children is best.*

**4** Answer the questions about the essay.

1 Does the writer cover everything in the task?
................................................................
2 What subjects other than home life and money does the writer mention? ................................................
3 Does the writer mention any of your ideas from exercise 2? ................................................................

**5** Read the essay title below and add some information for each note.

---

Living at home with your parents is the best time of your life. Do you agree?

**Notes**
Write about:
1 home life
2 responsibilities
3 ................................................ (your own idea)

---

**6** Write your answer to the question in 140–190 words. Use your notes and give reasons for your point of view.

The family unit  **47**

# 12 Making a difference

## VOCABULARY  Communication and effect

**1** Match the verbs with the definitions.

1 amuse ......
2 cheer up ......
3 congratulate ......
4 express ......
5 inspire ......
6 persuade ......
7 promote ......
8 stimulate ......

a encourage to grow or become active
b make someone feel or react in a particular way
c make someone feel happier
d make someone smile or laugh
e show thoughts or feelings with words or actions
f advertise
g tell someone that you are pleased that they have done something good
h make someone agree to do something

**2** Complete the sentences with the correct form of one of the verbs from exercise 1.

1 Most of the audience laughed at his joke, but I wasn't ........................... at all.
2 We are putting up posters to ........................... our band's first ever performance.
3 Tonia looks sad. Let's do something to ........................... her ........................... .
4 What is the government doing to ........................... the economy?
5 I spent ages trying to ........................... Jenny to come with us, but she refused.
6 He finds it difficult to ........................... himself in words, but he's an amazing painter.
7 I'd like to ........................... you on winning first prize in the essay competition.
8 This film ........................... a lot of people to have a more optimistic view of life.

**3** Complete the sentences so that they are true for you.

1 I'm often amused when ...........................
2 ........................... always cheers me up.
3 The last time I was congratulated was when ...........................
4 My favourite way to express myself is ...........................
5 I'm inspired by ...........................
6 Nobody will ever persuade me to ...........................

## READING

**1** Juan Mann, the inventor of the 'Free Hugs' movement, is about to appear on national TV. Read the introduction. How do you think he feels about becoming famous?
...........................

**2** Read the interview and put the questions in the correct place. One question is not needed.

a Do you get recognised even when you're not doing your free hugs?
b Is that why you go by the false name Juan Mann?
c How did this all start, Juan?
d How do you feel when you give someone a hug?
e What do you do when you're not giving out free hugs?
f So are you worried about how this fame is going to affect your life?

**3** Read the interview again and answer the questions.

1 What word best describes how Juan felt when he came back from London: lonely or pessimistic?
...........................

2 How did Juan feel when he first tried giving free hugs in the shopping mall? Was he afraid he would be misunderstood or nervous but optimistic?
...........................

3 Does he like giving free hugs to strangers because it is a relaxing thing to do or because it gives him a sense of achievement?
...........................

4 What are his feelings about becoming famous? Does he hope it will make him rich or does he think nothing will change?
...........................

5 Does he use a false name to keep his activity secret from his family and friends or to put the focus on his actions?
...........................

6 What word best describes Juan's personality? Is he warm or ambitious?
...........................

# Spreading the love

Today *GladMagz* is talking to Juan Mann, the inventor of the Free Hugs phenomenon. He is set to be interviewed on national TV tomorrow night, and he's feeling pretty nervous.

**GladMagz:** ¹ .......

**Juan Mann:** I came back from London in January 2004 and my family and friends were spread across the world. I was the only person I knew and I was all alone. My parents had divorced, I had broken up with my fiancée and my grandmother was sick and I needed to feel happy. I went out to a party one night and a completely random person came up to me and gave me a hug. I felt like a king! Six months later I decided to give away free hugs. It was kind of strange walking up to a stranger without any form of introduction, and I didn't want to bother anyone, so that's why I held up my 'Free Hugs' sign. My first hug was from a little old lady. I'd been standing with my sign for 15 minutes and I was terrified. But I'd been hoping that maybe one person out there would take me up on the offer, and the old lady did.

**GM:** ² .......

**JM:** Oh, I just have a little job around the corner from my house – nothing spectacular. I walk away from work and it's all just gone. I don't want to say where because I'm trying to keep work out of this whole thing – they're really excitable! It's very quiet around here; nothing much goes on and that's the way I like it. Giving free hugs is one thing that I've gone back to week after week without fail because I know I'm doing something. It doesn't matter that the money's not there and that it's not a career path, what matters is that it makes a difference to somebody's life just for a moment.

**GM:** ³ .......

**JM:** It is going to be interesting, but the important thing for me is being able to stay true to myself and keeping my job. People will notice me and I'll be a bit famous for a while but it will fade in the end. It's exciting but my life is just going to carry on as it always has and as it always will. If I became a rich and famous 'hugging celebrity' I would still be doing the same thing I do every week.

**GM:** ⁴ .......

**JM:** I keep my real name to myself because the whole thing about a different name is that it's not about me, it's about how it makes people feel and think. I used to say to my friends, 'I'm just one man! What can I do?!' I did feel that I was looking for something that was a little bit more than what's out there, I had to do something.

**GM:** ⁵ .......

**JM:** I cut my hair about a year ago because I was getting stopped and hugged at petrol stations while I was buying milk. I felt a bit like Superman and Clark Kent! This has grown beyond anything I ever thought was possible. What started out as a way for me to get a smile out of strangers has turned into this social theory of peace and humanity. I want to go on TV to say thank you to everybody.

---

**Word profile** *as*

**Choose the correct phrase.**

1 Global temperatures have risen *as a result of / as far as I know* industrial activity.
2 I think I write quite well. *As far as I know / As a matter of fact*, I've won several prizes for my essays.
3 You can go home when you like, *as a result of this / as far as I'm concerned*. I don't really care.
4 I'm not sure, but *as a matter of fact / as far as I know*, nobody has informed the head teacher about this.
5 *The Wanted* are the best band in the world, *as far as / as a matter of fact* my little sister is concerned.

## GRAMMAR The Passive (1): Review

**1** Rewrite the sentences in the passive. Use *by* if it is important to add who or what does something.

0 We may record your call.
   *Your call may be recorded.*

1 You use flour to make bread.
   ................................................................

2 They don't allow people under 15 to watch this film.
   ................................................................

3 Sunlight provides the power in this house.
   ................................................................

4 People in Brazil speak Portuguese.
   ................................................................

5 The neighbour's cat bit me on the leg.
   ................................................................

6 My brother will arrange everything.
   ................................................................

7 Somebody will give you instructions on arrival.
   ................................................................

8 People are spending more on smartphones than ever before.
   ................................................................

**2** Five of the eight underlined clauses in the text can be made passive. Choose which five and rewrite them in the passive.

<u>Last year I experienced real kindness</u> from a girl <u>who has since become my best friend</u>. I had to change school last summer because earlier in the year <u>Dad's company had moved him to an office in a different town</u>, and the rest of the family joined him. That was difficult for me – not only leaving my friends but the thought of having to make new friends. <u>People have often described me as shy</u> and it's true, I find it very difficult to be relaxed with new people. Anyway, on my first day at the new school, <u>someone was showing me into the building</u> when this girl came bouncing up to us and said, 'Hi, I'm Kate, your school buddy. <u>They've given me the job of making you feel welcome here.</u>' Kate stayed with me all day – <u>she sat with me in the lessons</u>, she explained how everything worked, she took me to lunch and introduced me to all her friends. <u>Her kindness really impressed me that day.</u>

1 ................................................................
2 ................................................................
3 ................................................................
4 ................................................................
5 ................................................................

**3** 👁 Correct the mistakes in these sentences or put a tick (✓) by any you think are correct.

1 I like to wear clothes which are from cotton.
   ................................................................

2 My bicycle has been stolen on 10th September.
   ................................................................

3 I have a lot of friends, but my best friend calls Maria.
   ................................................................

4 They eat special cakes which make for the wedding.
   ................................................................

5 I liked the festival very much and I think it should be held again next year. ................................................................

6 The first restaurant is specialised in seafood.
   ................................................................

## Causative

**4** Complete the sentences with the correct form of *have* or *get* and one of the verbs below.

| build | clean | cut | deliver | look |
| paint | take | take out | | |

1 I'm thinking of .............................. my bicycle .............................. pink. What do you think?

2 If your computer isn't working, why don't you .............................. Simon .............................. at it? He's good at that sort of thing.

3 You'll have to .............................. your photo .............................. if you're applying for a passport.

4 I couldn't afford to go to the hairdressers, so I .............................. my friend .............................. my hair.

5 I really need to .............................. my school coat .............................. . It's filthy!

6 She .............................. a tooth .............................. yesterday.

7 Mum couldn't be bothered to cook, so we .............................. a pizza .............................. to our house.

8 My friend's parents .............................. a swimming pool .............................. in their back garden.

**5** Imagine you are very rich. Write five things that you would have/get done for you every day.

*I'd have my meals cooked for me every day by a professional chef.*

................................................................
................................................................
................................................................
................................................................
................................................................
................................................................
................................................................
................................................................
................................................................

## VOCABULARY  both, either, neither

**1** Join the sentences with *both*, *either* or *neither*.

**0** He speaks French. He speaks Spanish.
   *He speaks both French and Spanish.*

**1** You can have a cake. But if you have a cake, you can't have a biscuit.
   ...............................................................

**2** I don't like cats. I don't like dogs.
   ...............................................................

**3** The film was funny. The film was also frightening.
   ...............................................................

**4** Maria doesn't have any time. Donna doesn't have any time.
   ...............................................................

**5** Maybe Greg is lying. Or maybe Dave is lying.
   ...............................................................

**6** He doesn't speak French. He doesn't speak Spanish.
   ...............................................................

**2** Make five sentences about you and one other person. Use *both … and* or *neither … nor*.
   *Both my brother and I hate football.*
   ...............................................................
   ...............................................................
   ...............................................................
   ...............................................................
   ...............................................................

## LISTENING

**1** Read the questions. What is each one asking you to listen for? Choose from this list.

|  | Question |
|---|---|
| main topic | ............... ............... |
| speaker's purpose | ............... |
| speaker's feeling | ............... |
| speaker's opinion | ............... |
| a detail in the situation | ............... ............... |
| a reason for something | ............... |

### EXAM TIPS

**Listening Part 1**
- Remember that each recording is repeated before the next question comes.
- Underline key words in the options and predict what you might hear.
- Listen to the whole extract before choosing your answer, as a question may focus on its general idea or purpose.
- Check your answers when you listen the second time.

**2** You will hear people talking in eight different situations. Read the questions, and underline the main ideas that might help you get the correct answers.

**1** You hear a girl talking about her summer job. How did she feel about it?
   A  enthusiastic
   B  uninterested
   C  confused

**2** You hear a radio announcement about a youth circus. What are listeners being invited to?
   A  a performance
   B  a party
   C  a talk

**3** You hear a girl talking about a race she's just won. What does she say about it?
   A  She was disappointed by it.
   B  She didn't have a chance to celebrate it.
   C  She was too exhausted to enjoy it.

**4** You hear a TV producer talking about his favourite TV show. Why does he like the show?
   A  It is romantic.
   B  It is funny.
   C  It is sad.

**5** You hear a journalist talking about his early career. Why is he telling the story?
   A  to point out that formal training is necessary these days
   B  to say that it's important to get on well with the editor
   C  to show that he was already a talented journalist

**6** You hear two friends talking about a school event. What is the boy doing?
   A  expressing a worry
   B  defending a decision
   C  refusing an invitation

**7** You hear a young woman talking about rock-climbing. Why does she do it?
   A  It gives her a sense of achievement.
   B  It satisfies her need to be alone.
   C  It lets her escape her daily routine.

**8** You hear a girl telling a friend about a problem she has with her phone. What does the girl decide to do?
   A  suggest her parents buy her a new phone
   B  buy a new phone herself
   C  ask the shop to sort out the problem

**3** ▶7  Listen. For questions 1–8, choose the best answer (A, B or C).

**4** ▶7 Listen again and check your answers.

Making a difference

# 13 Leading the way

## VOCABULARY  Leadership and achievement

**1** Complete the table with the words below. Some words can go in two columns.

adventurous   appreciation   cautious
criticism   doubt   fairly   influence   motivated
stand out   strict   sympathetic   target

| Noun | Adjective |
|---|---|
|  |  |
|  |  |

| Verb | Adverb |
|---|---|
|  |  |
|  |  |

**2** Match the words from exercise 1 to the definitions.
1 willing to try new and difficult things ............................
2 something that you try to achieve ............................
3 in a right and reasonable way ............................
4 the power to affect a person's behaviour ............................
5 taking care to avoid danger ............................
6 when you say that someone/something is bad ............................
7 feel uncertain about something ............................
8 be better than other similar things ............................
9 making sure rules are not broken ............................
10 keen to succeed ............................
11 understanding and caring ............................
12 when you understand how good something is ............................

**3** Complete the sentences with words from exercises 1 and 2.
1 Do you ever ............................ your ability to succeed?
2 Sara really wants to be the best student in school – she's the most ............................ person I know.
3 Don't be so ............................ . You have to take risks sometimes!
4 Have you set yourself a ............................ to achieve before the end of the year?
5 He's a talented writer, but he doesn't accept ............................ from anyone – even when he is wrong!
6 This essay is boring – you should try to be more ............................ in your thinking.
7 The audience showed their ............................ by standing up and applauding for over a minute.
8 I also have trouble sleeping at night, so I am very ............................ about your problem.

**4** Answer the questions about you.
1 Who is the most adventurous person you know?
.................................................................................
2 What keeps you motivated to work hard at school?
.................................................................................
3 Which person has the biggest influence on your life?
.................................................................................
4 Who in your class stands out from the crowd?
.................................................................................
5 In what situations are you happy in your own company?
.................................................................................

## READING

### EXAM TIPS

**Reading and Use of English Part 6**
- Read the text quickly for its general meaning and read the sentences A–G, underlining the important words.
- Look at the sentences in the text before and after the gaps to find possible links with the sentences A–G.
- Read through the whole text with your answers in place to check it makes sense.

**1** Read the article and underline pronouns and phrases which could be connected to something in the missing sentences in exercise 2. Look at the sentences before and after the gap. The first one has been done for you.

**2** 🔴 Choose from the sentences A–G the one which fits each gap 1–6. There is one extra sentence which you do not need to use.

A What the leader says must be followed, failure must be punished and positive results celebrated.
B To be seen as a good leader, the main thing is to meet the expectations of your followers.
C They are more interested in personal success or fame than in working hard as part of a team to achieve something great.
D Individuals who are well-trained and know what they are doing are more than capable of managing themselves and are very motivated.
E This means little more than having encouraging chats about their performance, and giving clear goals for them to work towards.
F It is important, of course, but not always as crucial as people might think.
G There is nothing more frustrating than a bad leader who can't make decisions or upsets people.

# WHAT TYPE OF LEADER COULD YOU BE?

Do you prefer to have a caring and helpful teacher or a strict and disciplined one? Do you think that only certain types of personality and styles of leadership achieve good results? The reality is that different situations require different leadership styles, often from the same person. Professor André Spicer and Professor Mats Alvesson have been researching various methods of leadership for a new book.

Whether you're a student organising a school project, the manager of a sports club, or the President of the United States, everyone is aware of the importance of good leadership skills. ▢ 1 But why do such situations occur, and what exactly do we mean by the term 'leader'? In fact, is having a leader or being one always the best solution?

'I am a leadership realist,' explains Prof. Spicer. ▢ 2 To take one example, for some people, offering to take the lead on a school project or at a sports event is just an easy way to avoid doing the boring or physically demanding tasks that are often necessary.

While researching the book six leader types were identified. Interestingly, they are not all positive. Three of the six are quite negative – the 'robot', the 'bully' and the 'commander'. Someone who is a 'commander' might have the right personality to join the military, for example. ▢ 3 But this attitude doesn't inspire people who do not share the view that this is the best way to get things done. The three positive leadership types are known as the 'saint', the 'gardener' and the 'friend'. These leaders all make sure that everyone is happy in their role, and feels part of the group.

Everyone has their own ideas about the best way to lead others, but the most important factor is that the leader and their followers share their idea of good leadership. You need to have different styles of leadership for different situations. ▢ 4 So, for example, there is no point in being a 'friend' in a situation which requires a 'commander'.

Being a good leader then is essentially about responding to the situation, and addressing the needs of the group. ▢ 5 Why then, do we often admire people who are perhaps great or famous leaders? It seems that our ideas about the importance of leadership are unrealistic, and some people like to show they can lead just to be popular rather than to actually help people or solve problems.

This has been recognised amongst university students, who have all grown up with the idea they can, and should, be important leaders. ▢ 6 Professor Spicer finds this odd: 'I wonder why the idea of being a follower is not more attractive – I think it is more positive, more realistic. It is achievable for all.'

**3** Find words or phrases in the text which mean the following.

1 having knowledge or experience of something (paragraph 2)
..................................

2 make someone feel that they want to do something and can do it (paragraph 4)
..................................

3 one of the things that has an effect on a situation, decision, event, etc. (paragraph 5)
..................................

4 relating to the most important characteristics or ideas of something (paragraph 6)
..................................

### Word profile *lead*

Match the meaning of *lead* in these sentences to the correct definition.

1 We need someone to **lead** this team, or we will never win anything. ......
2 At half-time, Brazil were **leading** by three goals. ......
3 One of the world's **leading** climate scientists is giving a talk here tonight. ......
4 I just want to **lead** a quiet life in the country. ......
5 My clever idea **led** to the company making lots of money. ......
6 The footpath **leads** directly to the river. ......

a be in control of
b best
c ahead
d cause something to happen
e goes in the direction of
f live in a particular way

## GRAMMAR  The passive (2): Other structures

**1** Complete the second sentence so that it has a similar meaning to the first sentence, using the word given. Do not change the word given. You must use between two and five words, including the word given.

**0** You must give everyone enough time to finish.
**GIVEN**
Everyone ......*must be given*...... enough time to finish.

**1** They're always making me do the boring jobs.
**BEING**
I'm ........................................ the boring jobs.

**2** To be given the chance of a leading role in a Hollywood film is Amy's dream.
**OFFERED**
Amy dreams ........................................ a leading role in a Hollywood film.

**3** You must submit your projects by Friday.
**HANDED**
Your projects ........................................ by Friday.

**4** Most people think that the new proposals are an improvement.
**GENERALLY**
The new proposals ........................................ an improvement.

**5** The judges told David about the prize before they told anyone else.
**FIRST**
David ........................................ told about the prize.

**6** The camp leaders might stop under-18s from going on the climbing trip.
**ALLOWED**
Under-18s ........................................ go on the climbing trip.

**2** Complete the paragraph with the verbs in brackets in the correct form.

I've recently started at a new school where students in their final year can [1] ........................... (reward) for years of good behaviour by [2] ........................... (give) more responsibility. This involves mainly helping younger students with problems, but it is also possible for other students [3] ........................... (punish) by the 'student officers' if they notice any discipline issues. Now, I'm sure most students appreciate [4] ........................... (help) sometimes, but no one really wants [5] ........................... (tell) what to do, or punished, by another student. It depends on the student to a great extent, though – you can see that some of them positively enjoy [6] ........................... (hand) the opportunity to act as teachers in some ways!

## EXAM TIPS

**Reading and Use of English Part 4**
- Read each first sentence carefully and think about its meaning.
- Read your completed second sentence to check that your answer means the same as the first sentence.
- Make sure you have not changed the word that is given.

**3** Correct the mistakes in these sentences or put a tick (✓) by any you think are correct.

**1** It will save a lot of electricity as solar energy is used. ...........................
**2** As could be seen, bikes are really very good: cheap, fast and healthy. ...........................
**3** I believe that this question can be looked at from several points of view. ...........................
**4** It will be prepare by our school cook. ...........................

## VOCABULARY  Phrasal verbs with *up*

**1** Complete the sentences with the verbs below in the correct form.

| come | keep | live | make | set | speak | turn |

**1** The company was ........................... up in 2012.
**2** Slow down! I can't ........................... up with you.
**3** For homework this week we have to ........................... up a story.
**4** A strange woman ........................... up to me and started talking.
**5** That film just about ........................... up to my expectations.
**6** ........................... up! I can't hear you.
**7** How many people ........................... up to the party last night?

**2** Rewrite the underlined parts of the sentences using phrasal verbs from exercise 1.

**0** Jo's **starting** a publishing company on the internet.
......*Jo's setting up a publishing company.*......

**1** I believed his story, but it turns out he **invented** the whole thing!
........................................

**2** What a wonderful show! It **met** all my expectations.
........................................

**3** He speaks so quickly that it is hard to **follow** him.
........................................

**4** The policeman **approached** me and asked me for my name and address.
........................................

**5** You'll have to **talk more loudly** because the microphone isn't working properly.
........................................

**6** I thought they weren't coming, but they eventually **arrived** an hour late.
........................................

## WRITING  An informal letter

See Prepare to write box, Student's Book page 23.

**1** Read the exam task below. How many questions does Bobbi ask?

..............................

> You have received this letter from your English-speaking friend Bobbi.
>
> What are you doing over the summer holidays? I'm thinking of applying for a job here as a leader at an international camp for children. I need some advice from you on what I should include in my application! What qualities do you think the camp would be looking for in a leader? Do you think my English is good enough to work in an international camp? What else should I say?
> Hope to hear from you soon.
> Bobbi

**2** Read the letter, ignoring gaps 1–10 for the moment. Has the writer answered all of Bobbi's questions?

> Hi Bobbi
>
> What a great idea! It would be fun to work in an international camp. I'm sure you'd make an excellent leader as you are so ¹.............................. to do your best in everything. Besides that, you wouldn't behave too ².............................. with the children, but let them enjoy themselves within the camp rules.
>
> You needn't worry about your level of English – it's fine and, what's more, you have a very ³.............................. accent, so everyone will understand what you say. I wish I could speak a foreign language as ⁴.............................. as you do.
>
> I think the ⁵.............................. thing to stress in your application is your knowledge of looking after kids. For instance, you've done babysitting on a ⁶.............................. basis for a while now, haven't you? You could also explain why you think you would make a good leader. I'm sure the job will require long hours, so describe yourself as '⁷..............................
> ⁸..............................' – but always cheerful!
>
> Last but not least, you could also talk ⁹.............................. about your love of sport and music, as both are very ¹⁰.............................. to this kind of work. Why not offer to bring your own guitar?
> Good luck – I hope you get the job!
> Love, Max

## EXAM TIPS

**Writing Part 2 (an informal letter)**
- Read the Part 2 question carefully, including the extract from the friend's letter.
- Spend a few minutes making notes about what to write about.
- Organise your letter clearly in paragraphs.
- Use informal language and include suitable adjectives and adverbs.

**3** Complete the letter with the adjectives and adverbs below.

| clear | enthusiastically | essential |
|---|---|---|
| extremely | fluently | hard-working |
| motivated | regular | relevant | strictly |

**4** Read the letter again. What is covered in each paragraph?

a Bobbi's ability in English  paragraph .......
b Bobbi's free-time interests  paragraph .......
c encouragement for Bobbi  paragraph .......
d Bobbi's skills and experience  paragraph .......

**5** Find linking phrases in the letter that mean the same as 1–4 below. There is one in each paragraph.

1 finally  ..............................
2 for example  ..............................
3 apart from  ..............................
4 another thing  ..............................

**6** Now answer the letter task in exercise 1 in your own words. Follow the advice in the Exam tip and remember to include a range of adjectives and adverbs. Write 140–190 words.

Leading the way

# 14 Getting there

## VOCABULARY  Phrasal verbs

**1** Complete the crossword, using the clues below.

**Across**

4 We'd better stop and let the engine … down; it's getting too hot.
6 In a car, you should … off when the traffic light turns green.
8 This train is going to pull … of the station in two minutes.
9 I don't know where to go so we must … up with Louis in the car in front.
11 Oh no! I think I've just … over some glass.

**Down**

1 … down! The speed limit is only 50 here.
2 There's a football match on today – that could … us up.
3 Something's wrong with the car. I think we're going to … down.
5 This fog is awful. I can hardly … out the car in front.
7 The train pulled … the station ten minutes late.
8 Did that car just pull … and the driver empty his rubbish bin?
10 Can you … up here for a minute while I get some cash?

**2** Match the phrasal verbs in exercise 1 to these definitions.

1 stop for a short time
2 stop working (of an engine)
3 become less hot
4 hit something with a moving vehicle
5 be able to see only with difficulty
6 travel at the same speed as
7 stop briefly at the side of something, e.g. the road
8 arrive at (of a train/car)
9 start to move (in a car)
10 leave (of a train/car)
11 reduce speed
12 delay

**3** Complete the sentences with the phrasal verbs.

1 Can you ………………………… ………………………… here please, driver. This is where I want to get out.
2 The train was ………………………… ………………………… because of a crash on the train line.
3 It was too foggy to ………………………… ………………………… the road signs.
4 ………………………… ………………………… ! You're driving too fast.
5 A driver ………………………… ………………………… next to me and asked me for directions.
6 Our cat was ………………………… ………………………… when it was running across the road.
7 I can't ………………………… ………………………… with you because you run too fast.
8 The bus driver ………………………… ………………………… a petrol station to fill up.
9 We were annoyed when the bus ………………………… ………………………… just as we turned the corner.
10 I'm too hot! Let's just sit in the shade and ………………………… ………………………… for a while.
11 Do you know what to do if your car ………………………… ………………………… ?
12 We've missed the train – it's ………………………… ………………………… of the station now.

## READING

**1** Read the definition of *ecotourism* in the first paragraph of the text. Choose the 'ecotourist' holiday below.

a a holiday organised by a large company in which a large group travels around, staying and eating in international hotels
b a holiday in which a few people explore a natural area with a local guide, staying in local accommodation
c a holiday to a resort that is staffed by people from all over the world and where you spend 14 days on the beach

**2** Match the aspects of ecotourism 1–7 to the paragraphs A–G.

1 It provides direct financial benefits for conservation.
2 It builds environmental awareness.
3 It provides financial benefits for local people.
4 It has very little negative impact.
5 It respects local culture.
6 It involves travel to natural destinations.
7 It supports human rights and democratic movements.

# ECOTOURISM – a definition

'Take only photographs, leave only footprints.' That was the golden rule for the responsible traveller in the past. But nowadays ecotourism is big business, and The International Ecotourism Society (TIES) has defined it as 'responsible travel to natural areas that encourages conservation of the environment and improves the welfare of local people.' Trips to exotic places are very popular with young people, who tend to be very environmentally aware. So what are the things to look for in a tour operator if you want your holiday to be truly green? According to TIES, there are several aspects to genuine ecotourism:

**A** These places are often remote areas, whether inhabited or uninhabited, and are usually under some kind of environmental protection scheme.

**B** Tourism causes damage. Ecotourism tries to reduce the negative effects of hotels, trails, and other things by using either recycled materials or local building materials, renewable sources of energy, recycling and safe disposal of waste, and environmentally sensitive architecture.

**C** Ecotourism means education, for both tourists and residents of nearby communities. Before departure tour operators should supply travellers with reading material about the country, environment and local people, as well as rules for both the traveller and the industry itself. This information helps prepare the tourist to learn about the places visited.

**D** Ecotourism helps raise money for environmental protection, research and education in a variety of ways, including park entrance fees, taxes on tour companies, hotels, airlines and airports, and voluntary donations.

**E** National Parks and other conservation areas will only survive if there are 'happy people' around their borders. The local community must be involved with and receive income and other benefits (clean water, roads, health clinics, etc.) from the conservation area and its tourist facilities.

**F** Ecotourism is not only 'greener' but also tries to be culturally sensitive and have a minimal effect on both the natural environment and the human population of a host country. This is not easy, especially since ecotourism often involves travel to remote areas where small and isolated communities have had little experience of interacting with foreigners.

**G** Although tourism is often seen as a tool for building international understanding and world peace, this does not happen automatically. Frequently, in fact, tourism helps the economies of undemocratic states. Mass tourism pays very little attention to the political system of the host country or struggles within it. Ecotourism is much more aware of the political situation.

Most tour operators who can truly be called ecotourism providers are trying to meet as many of these criteria as possible. This is very difficult for anyone operating eco-tours, and it is highly doubtful that any one project or operator can claim to meet them all. However, it does give a base of ideas to work from when looking into whether something is or isn't ecotourism.

## 3 Answer the questions about the article.

1 According to the article, what does ecotourism try to reduce?
..................................................
2 What two groups of people does ecotourism seek to educate?
..................................................
3 What two things benefit financially from ecotourism?
..................................................
4 What makes it difficult to be 'culturally sensitive'?
..................................................
5 How easy is it to find an ecotourism provider which covers all of the aspects listed here?
..................................................

## 4 Find words in the text which mean the following.

1 health and happiness (introduction) ..................
2 far away (A) ..................
3 unwanted things (B) ..................
4 money or goods given to help a person or organisation (D) ..................
5 talking or doing things with other people (F) ..................

## GRAMMAR  Reported speech

**1 Complete the sentences with the correct form of the verb.**

1 We can't help you.
   They told us they ............................ help us.
2 This is the first time I've tried prawns.
   Tom says that this ............................ the first time he ............................ prawns.
3 They're going to the new club next weekend.
   He told me they ............................ to the new club the next weekend.
4 The soup is much nicer when it's served hot.
   Sarah says the soup ............................ much nicer when it ............................ hot.
5 The original idea was not a practical one.
   Mark admitted that the original idea ............................ a practical one.

**2 Complete the reported speech statements.**

1 I won't be going on holiday this year.
   Sam says ............................................................
   ............................................................ .
2 She wanted to come to Kenya with us.
   He said she ............................................................
   ............................................................ .
3 I've always supported the idea of responsible tourism.
   She says ............................................................
   ............................................................ .
4 I'm organising a trip to Tibet.
   She said ............................................................
   ............................................................ .
5 I can arrange the whole thing for you.
   He told us ............................................................
   ............................................................ .
6 Fifty million tourists will be visiting Africa this year.
   She claims ............................................................
   ............................................................ .

**3 👁 Choose the correct sentence in each pair.**

1 a I tell him that you will arrive next week, but I don't think he understood.
   b I told him that you would arrive next week, but I don't think he understood.
2 a The officer said that we had to be quiet.
   b The officer told that we had to be quiet.
3 a It was about three o'clock and I asking the other people if they had seen my sister.
   b It was about three o'clock and I asked the other people if they had seen my sister.
4 a The officer said that David had forgotten to turn his camera off.
   b The officer told that David had forgotten to turn his camera off.

**4 Write the exact words that these people said.**

1 Ted says that air travel is going to get much more expensive.
   ' ............................................................ ,
2 She said she had enjoyed her holiday in Nepal very much.
   ' ............................................................ ,
3 Jade said she had been trying to reduce her carbon footprint.
   ' ............................................................ ,
4 The agent says that the best holidays aren't always the most expensive.
   ' ............................................................ ,
5 Polly said she would never forget the week she had spent in India.
   ' ............................................................ ,
6 Our teacher told us we'd never have a better opportunity to study abroad.
   ' ............................................................ ,

## VOCABULARY  Reporting verbs

**1 Match the verbs to the definitions below.**

1 agree       ......    5 insist      ......
2 confess     ......    6 persuade    ......
3 criticise   ......    7 point out   ......
4 enquire     ......    8 recommend   ......

a say that something or someone is bad
b admit to doing something bad
c say firmly that something is true
d make someone believe that something is true
e tell someone a piece of information
f advise that something should be done
g ask for information
h say that you will do something you have been asked to do

**2 Choose the correct reporting verb.**

1 My friends *persuaded* / *recommended* me to go to South America with them.
2 We *pointed out* / *criticised* that the hotel pool had been closed for most of the week.
3 James *insisted* / *confessed* to leaving the towels on the beach the day before.
4 The driver *agreed* / *enquired* to take us to the mountains for twenty dollars.
5 Sandra *persuaded* / *insisted* that she had packed the sun cream, but we couldn't find it anywhere.
6 Did you *point out* / *enquire* if under-18s were allowed to attend the quiz evening?

## LISTENING

**1** Have you ever stayed in a holiday resort? Make a list of the kinds of job the people who work there do.

......................................................................................
......................................................................................

**2** ▶8 You will hear five short extracts in which teenagers are talking about summer jobs in a holiday resort. Which speaker enjoys their job the most?

..................

**3** ▶8 Listen carefully to Speaker 1 again and choose from A–H what the speaker says about their job at the holiday resort.

A  I need to be prepared for the unexpected.
B  It can be boring at times.
C  I'm finding it easier than I did at first.
D  I have to be sociable most of the time.
E  It's good practice for my intended career.
F  It's more enjoyable than my previous jobs.
G  I enjoy certain tasks more than my colleagues.
H  The fixed routine is the best thing about it.

Speaker 1 [ 1 ]
Speaker 2 [ 2 ]
Speaker 3 [ 3 ]
Speaker 4 [ 4 ]
Speaker 5 [ 5 ]

**4** Now look at what Speaker 1 says. Underline the words that gave you the answer.

> I help with the entertainment in the resort, which covers the nightly stage shows, daily talks and exhibitions, and talent contests. Basically, I'm the person who has to make sure that everything runs smoothly, whether this means finding extra bottles of water for the bands or helping a guest to choose a costume for the talent show. It's impossible to have a daily routine because every day is different – I never get bored! And I seldom get a moment to myself. A major part of my job is to mix with the guests, and everyone knows me by the end of the week. If I'm not actually making announcements on stage, I'm chatting or dancing in the audience. It's all part of what I do.

### EXAM TIPS

**Listening Part 3**
- Listen to each speaker in full before trying to answer the question.
- Note your answer in pencil if you aren't sure after you listen the first time.
- Listen to the other speakers before you decide – this often makes it clearer when you listen again.

**5** ▶8 ● Now listen to Speakers 2–5 and choose from the list in exercise 3 what each speaker says about their job at the holiday resort. Use the letters only once. There are three extra letters which you do not need to use. Note any answers you aren't sure of.

**6** ▶8 Listen to all the speakers again. Did you change your mind for any of the answers?

### Word profile *break*

Choose the correct words to complete the sentences.
1 She broke the biscuit *in two / off* and gave one piece to her dog.
2 I'm training hard to break *the ice / the record* I set last summer.
3 You can trust her. She has never broken *a record / an agreement*.
4 He is in trouble with the police for breaking *the law / the ice*.
5 It broke my *heart / promise* when I heard the tragic news.
6 Let's play a game to break *off / the ice*.
7 I hope we don't have to break *in two / off* our holiday early again this year!

Getting there

# 15 The bigger picture

## VOCABULARY  Global issues: nouns and verbs

**1** Complete the words in the table, then add the missing words.

|   | Noun | Verb |
|---|------|------|
| 1 | b a n | ban |
| 2 | c ... ll ... ct ... n | |
| 3 | | c ... p ... r ... t |
| 4 | | cr ... t ... c ... s |
| 5 | ... l ... ct ... n | |
| 6 | | s ... pp ... rt |

**2** Match the verbs in the table to the definitions.

1 say that something or someone is bad  ..........................
2 ask people to give money for something  ..........................
3 choose by voting  ..........................
4 forbid  ..........................
5 work together  ..........................
6 actively agree with a person or idea  ..........................

**3** Complete the sentences with the correct form of a word from exercise 1.

1 She's .......................... for charity.
2 He's talking to his .......................... . 
3 Speaking Spanish .......................... in this classroom – English only! 
4 We have an annual .......................... for president of the Students' Union. 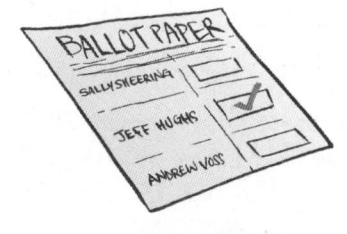
5 They'll be more successful if they .......................... with each other. 
6 She doesn't take .......................... very well. 

## READING

**1** Read the text 'Do we care about politics?', ignoring the gaps. Which sentence best summarises the main point of the text?

a Young people use social media more these days.
b Young people don't agree on many things these days.
c Young people are less involved in politics these days.

### EXAM TIPS

**Reading and Use of English Part 1**
- Always read the whole text first to understand its meaning.
- Look carefully at the words before and after each gap. Do any provide a clue to the answer?
- If you don't know the answer, try to decide which options do not fit the gap and choose a different one.
- Read the whole text through again to check it makes sense.

**2** Read the text and decide which answer (A, B, C or D) best fits each gap. There is an example at the beginning (0).

| 0 | A | took | B | caught | C | made | D | held |
| 1 | A | bag | B | thing | C | case | D | happening |
| 2 | A | credit | B | success | C | win | D | gain |
| 3 | A | way | B | event | C | condition | D | situation |
| 4 | A | decline | B | refusal | C | descent | D | dive |
| 5 | A | animated | B | busy | C | energetic | D | motivated |
| 6 | A | classic | B | standard | C | traditional | D | acceptable |
| 7 | A | lean | B | swing | C | favour | D | tend |
| 8 | A | shoot | B | throw | C | launch | D | set |

Unit 15

## DO WE CARE ABOUT POLITICS?

Gone are the days when students and young people in general **(0)** ..A.. an active interest in politics. Fewer young people vote in elections than used to be the **(1)** ......., and, while some young people still get involved, it would be considered a huge **(2)** ....... now if even 500 young people met to discuss a political issue. There is no shortage of causes for concern, so what is different about the **(3)** ....... today?

Sanal Batra leads the Students' Union at an Asian university. He gives several reasons for this **(4)** ....... in number and importance: nowadays, students appear to be **(5)** ....... with their own lives, and social media such as Facebook and Twitter have made it easy for them to express their thoughts. Also, he says, young people don't feel part of the **(6)** ....... establishment – they have no voice on the larger stage, so **(7)** ....... to focus more on small issues that affect them directly.

Yet this is not necessarily a bad thing, Sanal says. Many students have used social media networks to learn about problems and even **(8)** ....... specific campaigns against issues that may have an impact on society.

## DO WE CARE ABOUT CHARITIES?

According to one study, social media can also have an unfortunate effect on both political involvement and charities. The study shows that Facebook and Twitter users are happy to show their support for causes with a 'Like' or a re-Tweet – but then contribute nothing financially. This could be because they are using social media as a means to show others how generous and fashionable they are without having to put their hands in their pockets.

Report author Kirk Kristofferson said, 'Our research shows that if people are able to declare support for a charity publicly in social media it can actually make them less likely to donate to the cause later on.' It appears that social media campaigns do raise awareness but that could be at a cost to how much is raised from collecting money in the high street. Mr Kristofferson argued, 'If the goal is to generate real support, social media campaigns may be a mistake.'

**3** Now read the rest of the text, and complete the summary sentences below (about both texts).

1 Yong people are less likely to be politically motivated these days because ....................................................
....................................................

2 However, they do get more involved with ....................
....................................................

3 Equally, they support charities in a different way as
....................................................

4 So, using social media to promote charities may be a mistake because ....................................................
....................................................

**4** Find words or phrases in the 'charities' text which mean the following.

1 influence something in a negative way (paragraph 1) ...........................
2 give something, especially money, in order to provide or achieve something with other people (paragraph 1) ...........................
3 announce something publicly or officially (paragraph 2) ...........................
4 cause something to exist (paragraph 2) ...........................

### Word profile *key*

Match the sentences to the meanings of the word *key*.

1 I **keyed** in my username and password. ........
2 If you don't know the answer, check the **key**. ........
3 The **key** ingredient for a successful party is inviting the right people. ........
4 The **key** to success is hard work. ........
5 I'm locked out and the neighbour doesn't have a spare **key**. ........
6 Thr is on **ky** on my kyboard which is brokn. ........

a piece of metal used for opening or closing a lock
b list of answers to questions
c way to achieve something
d part of a keyboard
e very important in influencing or achieving something
f put information into a computer using a keyboard

## GRAMMAR  Modals (3): Deduction

**1** Complete the sentences with *must* or *can't* and the correct form of the verbs in brackets.

1  Daniel came first in the marathon! He ............................................ (train) really hard this summer.
2  Our new head teacher looks very young. She ............................................ (be) more than 30 years old.
3  It's really cold outside. It ............................................ (snow) on the mountains.
4  Oh, hello. You ............................................ (be) Ally's brother. Nice to meet you.
5  Pete trapped his finger in the car door. That ............................................ (hurt)!
6  Well, I arrived at 8.05 and they weren't there. They ............................................ (wait) for very long.
7  You ............................................ (be) delighted when you heard that you'd been offered the job.
8  You ............................................ (see) Molly when you were in town, because she's on holiday in America. It ............................................ (be) someone who looks like her.

**2** Rewrite the sentences with the verbs in brackets.

0  I'm sure he's at work today. (must)
   He *must be at work today.*
1  Maybe John didn't know about the party. (might)
   John ..................................................................
2  Perhaps Janet forgot to tell you about it. (could)
   Janet ..................................................................
3  It's not possible that this is your bag. (can't)
   This ..................................................................
4  Perhaps they met when they were on holiday? (may)
   They ..................................................................
5  I'm certain that I've seen this film before. (must)
   I ..................................................................
6  It's possible that the children missed the early train. (might)
   The children ..................................................................
7  There's no way that was the first time he's played tennis. (can't)
   That ..................................................................
8  It's possible that Alex is still in class. (might)
   Alex ..................................................................

**3** 👁 Correct the mistakes in these sentences or put a tick (✔) by any you think are correct.

1  It must be very interesting. ............................
2  It can go wrong, but it can go right too, and if it does it was worth the effort. ............................
3  We wouldn't be able to do 80 km on Saturday because in the mountains it is very difficult and we can get lost. ............................
4  My supposed friend turned around and said, 'I don't know you sir, you might have confused me with someone else.' ............................
5  Obviously, it's wonderful to go to a zoo and see the animals from different countries all together, but it mustn't be very nice to be disturbed all day and to have no freedom. ............................
6  There are great views throughout the ride, there's an astonishing castle and also a butterfly farm that can turn out to be very interesting. ............................

## VOCABULARY  Phrases with *in*

**1** Complete the word puzzle.

1  in ........ = considering the whole of something
2  in ........ = happening or being done now
3  in ........ = without telling other people
4  in ........ = one after another
5  in ........ = as a total amount
6  in ........ = where everyone can see or hear

**2** Complete the sentences with the phrases from exercise 1.

1  I don't want to talk about our business ............................ . What if someone hears us?
2  We haven't finished decorating yet. Work is still ............................ .
3  The head teacher called each of the boys to her office ............................ .
4  My head hurts, I'm tired, I'm hungry – ............................ , I'm feeling pretty bad.
5  We collected £265 ............................ for the charity.
6  They held the meeting ............................ , because they didn't want anyone to know about it.

Unit 15

## WRITING  A review (1)

See Prepare to write box, Student's Book page 79.

**1 Read the exam task and answer the questions.**

1 What do you have to write a review about? ................
..............................................................................
2 Where will it appear? ..................................................
3 Who will read it? .........................................................
..............................................................................
4 What information should you include in your review?
..............................................................................

You see the following advert on a website called movielove.com

> **Film reviews wanted**
> We're looking for reviews of films for our readers all over the world! Have you seen something recently that you could review for us? Tell us what the film was about, and describe its good and bad points. Would you recommend it to our readers? The best reviews will be published on this website.

Write your **review**.

### EXAM TIPS

**Writing Part 2 (a review)**
- Answer all the points or questions in the task.
- Write about both the positive and negative aspects of what you are reviewing.
- Give your own opinion at the end, and a recommendation if appropriate.
- Remember that you can invent a film (book, etc.) for your review if you want to.

**2 Read the film review quickly. Without putting the paragraphs in the correct order, can you tell if it is positive or negative?** ...........................

**3 Put the paragraphs in the correct order according to these general topics.**

Introducing the film ....... The negative parts .......
The positive parts ....... The conclusion .......

**4 Did the writer of the review answer all the questions in the task?** ............

**5 Make the text more interesting by replacing the words in bold with these more descriptive expressions. (Write them in the brackets.)**

> absolutely determined    highly original
> quite witty    really hilarious    totally crazy

**6 Now write your own review in 140–190 words. Use the structure in exercise 3 to guide you.**

## JUST VOTE ★★★★★

**A** In general, I'd thoroughly recommend this **unusual** (....................................) film to anyone with a sense of humour. If you like comedy, you'll love this classic.

**B** The idea for the film might not sound too exciting to you, but believe me, it's a **very funny** (....................................) comedy that will make you laugh so hard it hurts. The script is fast-paced and **amusing** (....................................), the lead actors are brilliant, and the music – a mix of indie pop and rap – really fits the film.

**C** A film I saw recently was Just Vote! It's set in a high school in the United States and it's about the election campaigns of two students who both want to be president of the students' union. The two candidates are very different. They are both **keen** (....................................) to win the election, and their attempts to increase their popularity become **sillier** (....................................) as the film goes on.

**D** The only weak part of the film was the ending. I don't want to spoil it for you by saying exactly what happens, but I will say that it was a bit too 'Hollywood' for me. Why must they always have an emotional ending?

The bigger picture  63

# 16 New and improved!

## VOCABULARY   Advertising: nouns and verbs

**1** Match the words and phrases to the definitions.

1. commercial break   .......
2. sample   .......
3. on offer   .......
4. consumer   .......
5. launch   .......
6. sponsor   .......
7. logo   .......
8. aimed at   .......

a  a person who buys something for their own use
b  the time on TV or radio used for advertising
c  support a person/organisation financially as a way of advertising
d  a small amount of something that shows you what it's like
e  on sale at a cheaper price than usual
f  intended to influence or affect a particular person or group
g  a design or symbol used by a company to advertise its products
h  make available for the first time

**2** Choose the correct answer.

1. A local company has just decided to *sponsor* / *launch* our band.
2. That car manufacturer apparently spent $1 million on their new *consumer* / *logo*.
3. I refuse to buy anything that is really *on offer* / *aimed at* children.
4. The best thing about some TV programmes is the *logos* / *commercial breaks*.
5. There were people in the shopping centre giving out *logos* / *samples* of a new breakfast cereal.
6. The new edition of Minecraft was *launched* / *sponsored* yesterday.

**3** Complete the sentences with words and phrases from exercise 1.

1. We need to design a new ............................. for our clothing company.
2. Did you receive a ............................. of our new product in the post this week?
3. I don't usually buy biscuits, but they were ............................. at the supermarket today.
4. These food price increases will affect all ............................. .
5. I'm trying to find a new ............................. for the children's football team.
6. The company is ............................. its new product at the end of the month. It's ............................. the teenage market.

**4** Answer the questions about yourself.

1. What is your favourite brand of clothing?
2. What do you do during commercial breaks?
3. Who sponsors your favourite football team?
4. When did you last buy something that was on offer?
5. What was it?
6. What is your favourite logo?

## READING

**1** Have you ever thought about a career in advertising? Write five words describing what you think it would be like.

**2** Can you think of any myths about advertising? What are they?

> **myth (n):** an idea that is not true but is believed by many people

**3** Read the article on page 65. Does it mention any myths you thought of? Does the author have a positive or negative view of the advertising industry?

**4** Label each section in the article with the correct heading.

a  You'll make a fortune!
b  Advertising is the same as marketing.
c  It's a really exciting career.
d  Advertising is morally wrong.
e  Anyone can learn to sell.

# Five myths about advertising

**1:** ...........................................................................
No, it isn't! They're connected but different. Marketing is about finding out what customers want and using that information to design and create products that meet their needs. Advertising is about trying to persuade people to buy your products once you've created them. Advertisers don't make products, they sell them. So, working in advertising requires different skills from working in marketing.

**2:** ...........................................................................
Absolutely not! It's certainly true that training will help anyone to perform better in their work, but selling is a talent that you either have or you don't have. It's part of your personality. It's probably more accurate to say that someone who can sell, can sell anything – the skill is the same whatever the product. Training will make a good salesperson great, but it won't turn someone into a salesperson who doesn't have selling in their soul.

**3:** ...........................................................................
It can be, yes – if you're part of the team that creates a really successful advertisement, it can be a lot of fun and you'll get the sense of achievement that always results from doing something well. Just don't think it will be like that all the time – people in advertising work hard, they work long hours and they may not work at all if the product they're advertising doesn't sell. It's a tough industry to work in, there's a lot of competition and there's always someone who wants your job!

**4:** ...........................................................................
Well, you might, but it's never a good idea to go into a job thinking that it's an easy way to make money quickly. Think of the thousands of people working in advertising – some of them will become wealthy but most will not, as in any profession. You will need to be willing to work for a modest income while you're learning the job, perhaps for a number of years. With talent and perhaps a little luck, you may eventually earn a high salary.

**5:** ...........................................................................
There's nothing immoral or dishonest about advertising. The idea that selling is dishonest probably comes from the past, when sellers did not always tell the truth about the products they were selling. Today, advertising agencies must follow rules and there are severe penalties for any who do not. Advertising messages are often extremely sophisticated and may suggest that a product is better than it actually is, but it is illegal to make statements that are incorrect.

## 5 Answer the questions about the article.

1 What is the main difference between advertising and marketing?

2 Does the writer think that it's possible for anyone to learn to sell? Why / why not?

3 Why is advertising a tough industry to work in?

4 What are the key features that might make you wealthy if you work in advertising?

5 Why are advertisers generally honest these days?

## Word profile *no*

**Complete the beginnings of the sentences with the words below and match them with the endings.**

good   matter   need   wonder

1 There's no ............................... for you to help me; ........
2 It's no ............................... trying to send a text from here – ........
3 No ............................... how hard I tried, ........
4 It's no ............................... you're so fit – ........

a I couldn't come up with any ideas for the campaign.
b I can do it myself.
c you're always at the gym.
d there's no mobile phone signal.

## GRAMMAR  Conditionals (1): Review

**1** Complete the sentences with the verbs in brackets in the correct tense.

1. If I ........................... (hear) a noise in the night, I always get out of bed and check.
2. I feel tired if I ........................... (watch) too much television.
3. You ........................... (save) a lot of money tomorrow if you only buy things that are on offer.
4. Would you sponsor us if we ........................... (form) a volleyball team?
5. Ice cream ........................... (melt) if you leave it out of the freezer.
6. If I ........................... (win) a lot of money, I'd buy a new house.
7. You ........................... (have) an accident if you don't stop driving so fast.
8. I'd have slept better if I ........................... (not play) till late on the Xbox.
9. If the government ........................... (ban) advertising, they'd lose a lot of money.
10. If you had told me you were hungry, I ........................... (make) you a sandwich.

**2** Rewrite the sentences using the third conditional.

0. We didn't know Dan was in hospital, so we didn't visit him.
   If *we'd known Dan was in hospital, we'd have visited him.*
1. I loved the campaign, so I bought the product!
   If ...........................
2. The skirt wasn't on offer so she didn't buy it.
   If ...........................
3. I watched the film because I'd read a great review.
   I wouldn't ...........................
4. You didn't ask me to sponsor you, so I didn't.
   I would ...........................
5. She got the job because she asked all the right questions.
   If ...........................
6. They didn't sell their products because they didn't advertise.
   They would ...........................
7. I needed to go shopping, so I didn't go to the library.
   If ...........................
8. We didn't meet you at the cinema because we didn't know you were going.
   We would ...........................

**3** Correct the mistakes in these sentences or put a tick (✓) by any you think are correct.

1. You can go to the beach if the weather will be good. ...........................
2. Now I have a chance to prove myself, if you employ me. ...........................
3. I would be very pleased if you came and visit me. ...........................
4. Probably, if nothing would have happened, I would have lost anyway. ...........................

## VOCABULARY  Adverb + adjective collocations

**1** Complete the sentences with these adverbs.

| actively | automatically | conveniently | finely |
| naturally | nicely | warmly | well |

1. The hotel is ........................... located within walking distance of the beach.
2. First, take the ........................... chopped garlic and fry it gently in olive oil.
3. I was ........................... welcomed by my friend's parents when I stayed with them last weekend.
4. Tina is usually ........................... dressed – so why does she look so untidy today?
5. I'm not a ........................... talented singer, I'm afraid.
6. The weekend has a ...........................-balanced programme of activities.
7. A username will be ........................... generated when you fill in all your details.
8. My mother is ........................... involved in a campaign to ban advertising to children.

**2** Complete the second sentence using the correct form of the bold words.

1. **Scientists** have **proven** that this method works.
   This method has been ........................... .
2. There is an **automatic update** for this computer program.
   This computer program is ........................... .
3. As an artist, he is **recognised** all over the **globe**.
   He's a ........................... artist.
4. We use only materials which are considered to be **sound** from an **ecological** point of view.
   We use only ........................... materials.
5. I'd love to be **independent** as far as my **finances** are concerned.
   I'd love to be ........................... .
6. It's **incredible** how **economical** these electric cars are.
   They are ........................... .
7. This information needs **constant updating** to be useful.
   It needs to be ........................... .

## LISTENING

**1** You will hear an interview with a young woman talking about her job in advertising. Make notes on these questions.

What do you think she enjoys about the job?
..................................................................................
What are the most important qualities for a career in advertising?
..................................................................................

**2** Read questions 1–7 on the right. Underline the main idea of each question. The first one has been done.

### EXAM TIPS

**Listening Part 4**
- Underline the main idea in each question and the key words in each option.
- The questions are in the order you will hear them, and are usually introduced by a question from the conversation.

**3** ▶9 Listen to the first part of the interview and choose the correct answer to question 1.

**4** Now read part of the interview and underline the words which gave you the answer.

By chance, really. Um, I'd just graduated with a degree in psychology. As you can imagine, there aren't that many opportunities available in that field. And to be honest, I had a low opinion of the advertising industry at that time – you know: it's the business of lying to people to persuade them to buy things they don't need. But a friend of mine told me about a job available at the agency he was working at. I needed the money, so I applied – and soon grew to love it.

**5** What parts of the extract above might lead you to the wrong answer?

**6** ▶9 Listen to the rest of the interview and choose the best answer (A, B or C).

1 Tina <u>didn't want to go into advertising</u> at first because
  A she thought it was a dishonest business.
  B she wanted to be a psychologist.
  C she knew it was difficult to find a job.
2 What does Tina enjoy most about her work?
  A the opportunity to use her imagination
  B the personalities of her colleagues
  C the satisfaction of helping people
3 Tina does not enjoy her job when
  A she has to work on her own.
  B clients don't have a clear idea of their requirements.
  C there is a lot of pressure to complete a project on time.
4 How does she use a computer in her work?
  A to put together some initial ideas
  B to present a campaign to her bosses
  C to put the finishing touches to a campaign
5 Tina gets her ideas from
  A surfing the internet.
  B looking closely at a client's needs.
  C having meetings with her colleagues.
6 What does she look for in a new employee?
  A the ability to get on with others
  B a degree-level qualification
  C a wide variety of interests
7 When talking about her spare-time activity, Tina reveals
  A a desire to be a professional musician.
  B that she is very focused on her career.
  C a lack of concern for her personal finances.

**New and improved!**

# 17 Making headlines

## VOCABULARY  The media

**1** Match the two halves of the phrases.

1 keep
2 keep
3 celebrate
4 gossip
5 review
6 make
7 comment
8 highlight
9 chill

a about
b performances
c up to date with ...
d on current events
e the need for
f out
g you amused
h fun of
i achievements

1 ....... 2 ....... 3 ....... 4 ....... 5 .......
6 ....... 7 ....... 8 ....... 9 .......

**2** Complete the advert with the phrases, or parts of the phrases, from exercise 1.

### CHILL OUT

*Chill Out* is a new internet magazine by students, for students. You'll find plenty to keep you ¹............................. here – from ²............................. of the latest music downloads, to ³............................. on current events on campus. Every week there's a new profile of a well-known ex-student where we ⁴............................. their achievements since they left school. Our sports section will keep you up to ⁵............................. with the latest results, and our 'Public Eye' page will give you all the ⁶............................. about local celebrities. There are cartoons to ⁷............................. fun of public figures and, more seriously, a campaigns section where we ⁸............................. the need for change in university life. Visit us at www.chillout.ac.uk.

**3** Complete the sentences so that they are true for you.

1 I keep up to date with the news by .............................
   .............................
2 The best bit of celebrity gossip I know is .............................
   .............................
3 A TV show that makes fun of politicians in my country is called .............................
4 If I want to read a review of a film, I look at .............................
   .............................
5 When I want to chill out, I .............................

## READING

**1** What makes a good journalist? Write one important point, then read the article quickly to see if your point is included.

.............................
.............................

### EXAM TIPS

**Reading and Use of English Part 7**
- Always read the questions first and underline the main ideas in them.
- Read all the texts quickly for general meaning.
- If you don't understand a word or phrase in a text, try to work out its meaning from the rest of the sentence.
- Choose an answer for every question, even if you have to guess.

**2** 🔴 You are going to read an article in which young journalists give tips to other young people looking for a job in journalism. For questions 1–10, choose from the journalists (A–E). The journalists may be chosen more than once.

Which journalist

| | |
|---|---|
| recommends making stories as short as possible? | 1 |
| suggests writing about a variety of subjects before specialising? | 2 |
| mentions that joining the best team for you is crucial? | 3 |
| says never to turn down any job offer? | 4 |
| says you should always admit it when you do not know something? | 5 |
| emphasises the importance of telling the truth? | 6 |
| suggests putting a lot of effort into preparing for your first job? | 7 |
| says good writing can sometimes make the reader feel upset? | 8 |
| stresses the importance of factual accuracy? | 9 |
| recommends keeping up to date with current affairs? | 10 |

**3** Read the texts again and underline the parts of the text which gave you each answer.

68  Unit 17

## A Zach (writer for *The Chatterer*)

The most important thing I'm doing for my career is connecting with suitable people. Nothing in life is entirely about the individual, and if you don't find the right group to work with you'll never be happy. I work with great people and even on terrible days, I'm better off than I would be if I had decided to compromise. To me, great journalism answers important questions people didn't even know they wanted answers to. It translates the emotions of a situation so accurately and deeply that the reader has no choice but to feel them as though he or she was there. It leaves the reader in a better or worse place than he or she started, but never in the same place.

## B Tina (editor of *MaxRumors*)

If you want a career in journalism, say 'yes' to everything. Every job, however dull, gives you the chance to meet people. Don't worry too much about your first job – you need experience and it is important to remain open-minded as in the future, an employer will look less at the subject matter and more at your commitment to the task and your achievements. This is a hard industry to get into and you need to take any opportunity that arises. Good journalism is about knowing the full details. The more you research your subject and find new ways to capture events and news, then the better your journalism will be. Triple check sources and tips, and make sure you're always 100% sure before you hit the 'submit' button.

## C Nicky (managing editor of victornewssource.com)

The number one thing I stress with new writers is that every single word in a sentence should be meaningful. Don't write complicated sentences around the facts when you can just come right out and say what you mean. Using fewer words is often more powerful, especially on the web. Identify the story and push it as far as it can go. Readers can sense when you're half-hearted or bored, and they'll forget about you if you don't write every story with passion. Good journalism is all about honesty, even if it means being honest about being wrong.

## D Elizabeth (freelance multimedia journalist)

Be informed: read news, watch news, and don't just limit yourself to the media you agree with. You will produce better work more quickly, ask more relevant questions and have better ideas if you are more aware. There's nothing more embarrassing than a journalist who hasn't bothered to get the facts together and doesn't know what they're talking about. The most important thing I did for my career was to get relevant work experience at the start. It doesn't matter what you do when you begin – on your CV it shows you were interested and determined enough to get yourself there. I'm confident it was my unpaid job at the local newspaper that helped me get my first proper job in journalism and, as they say, the journey begins with that very first step.

## E Charlie (trainee sports editor for *The Trumpet*)

I didn't only focus on one area at first. I started writing short news stories about people in sport but also covered technology, and then moved to write about business too. Trying different things lets you find out what you're good at, and discover how different topics are covered. Always remember the five Ws (who, what, where, when, why). It's basic, but how you order information is essential to better writing. Also, don't be afraid to say you don't understand. Journalists spend their time talking to specialists. Better to ask a question at the time than feel foolish in print later on.

**4 Find words in the text which mean the following.**

1 agree to something which is not exactly what you want (A)
2 time and energy you are willing to give to a job (B)
3 significant, containing meaning (C)
4 related to what is useful or being talked about (D)
5 stupid (E)

## EP Word profile *date*

**Complete the sentences with the words and phrases below.**

back    from    out of    up to

1 This information dates .............................. 50 years.
2 I'm sorry, but your documents are .............................. date.
3 I have copies of this magazine dating .............................. 1999 to the present day.
4 It's important to keep your software .............................. date if you want to avoid problems.

## GRAMMAR  Conditionals (2): Mixed

**1** Match the beginnings and ends of the sentences.

1  If I hadn't bought that new laptop,  .......
2  The performance would have been a disaster  .......
3  I would have known what her problem was  .......
4  If I had brought my swimming costume,  .......
5  If I spent more time studying,  .......
6  You wouldn't have crashed the car  .......
7  You would be living in the United States now  .......
8  If I hadn't eaten those prawns,  .......

a  if you were a more confident driver.
b  if I was a doctor.
c  I would be able to afford a holiday now.
d  I wouldn't be feeling so ill now.
e  if you weren't such a good actor.
f  I might have done better in my exams.
g  if your father had taken that job with Microsoft.
h  I would be lying by the pool right now.

**2** Write mixed conditional sentences from the original sentences. Use *could* or *might* if you can.

0  I saw the film last week, so I know how it ends.
If ...I hadn't seen the film last week,...
...I wouldn't know how it ends...

1  He didn't bring his mobile phone. That's why he can't call for help.
If ..............................................................

2  I don't have a degree, so I wasn't able to apply for the teaching job.
I ..............................................................

3  Sandra doesn't enjoy horror films so she didn't come to the cinema with us.
Sandra ..............................................................

4  We lost the match. That's why we're unhappy now.
If ..............................................................

5  John never met the right person. That's probably why he isn't married now.
John ..............................................................

6  I'm not good at cooking, so I didn't become a chef.
If ..............................................................

7  They've got a new baby, so they didn't go on holiday in the summer.
They ..............................................................

8  You broke the living room window. You haven't got any pocket money left.
You ..............................................................

**3**  Correct the mistakes in these sentences or put a tick (✓) by any you think are correct.

1  I thought if I had failed, I wouldn't show my face to my family. .............................
2  I think that our way of life would be very different, if the telephone was not invented. .............................
3  They told me that I could go on the school trip, if I had asked my parents first. .............................
4  I'd have really liked to know what would have happened if you hadn't been there.
.............................
5  If the marlin could speak, it would have told the old man the same thing. .............................

## VOCABULARY  Phrasal verbs

**1** Match the phrasal verbs to the definitions.

1  get across  .......
2  follow up  .......
3  bring up  .......
4  look into  .......
5  catch up on  .......
6  leave out  .......
7  back up  .......
8  clear up  .......

a  introduce a particular subject
b  deal with a problem
c  make a person understand something
d  investigate
e  support
f  take further action
g  become up to date about something
h  not include

**2** Complete the sentences with the correct form of the phrasal verbs from exercise 1.

1  We have a great politics teacher who is very good at ............................ ideas ............................ to us.
2  Did you ever manage to ............................ those problems you were having with the mobile phone company?
3  The journalist ............................ his review of the book with an interview with the author.
4  I was fortunate that my family ............................ me ............................ when I decided to change my college course.
5  I'm writing an article for the school magazine which ............................ the question of whether exams are getting easier every year.
6  I don't want to be ............................ of this meeting – why am I not on the list?
7  I don't read the news when I'm on holiday, but I always try to ............................ it when we get home.
8  You have ............................ some interesting points. Let's discuss them later.

## WRITING  An essay (3)

See Prepare to write box, Student's Book pages 13, 57 and 89.

**1** Read the four paragraphs below quickly and put them in the correct order.

1 ……  2 ……  3 ……  4 ……

**A** ¹………………………, some journalists want to find sensational stories to sell. They're more interested in celebrities' private lives than in real news. They have been known to pursue someone and make their life a misery, for no reason other than famous people are considered not to have the right to privacy. Then, ²……………………… they write the story and public interest dies, they move on to their next victim.

**B** So, ³……………………… that I have presented the two sides of the argument, it is clear that journalism must find a balance between informing the public and respecting the privacy of individuals. We should consider, though, who buys the newspapers and supports these journalists.

**C** Journalists do an essential job. They expose important stories, including scandals, and also ensure that we know both sides of an issue. ⁴……………………… they do only that, everything works well.

**D** This is an important topic, especially ⁵……………………… the way some journalists behave, chasing celebrities around and using all sorts of unpleasant methods to get their photo or their story. But what is more important, the privacy of famous people or the journalists' role in keeping the public informed?

### EXAM TIPS

**Writing Part 1 (an essay)**
- Use a four-paragraph structure for the essay.
- Organise your ideas for and against the topic.
- Try to write in sentences of more than one clause and use a variety of linking words.

**2** Read the essay again and fill the gaps with these linking words.

> considering    However    now    once    Provided

**3** Choose the best title for the essay.
   **a** Journalists should respect individuals' privacy. Do you agree?
   **b** Celebrities should be protected from curious journalists. Do you agree?

**4** Think about what each paragraph in the essay does. Match the functions in the box below to the paragraphs.

Paragraph
1 ………………………
2 ………………………
3 ………………………
4 ………………………

> reacts to the idea in the title
> introduces the topic
> gives details of arguments against
> gives details of arguments for
> presents the other side of the argument
> refers back to the title
> summarises the two sides, possibly with a personal opinion

**5** Your English teacher has asked you to write an essay. Read the title and think of three points under each topic to include in your essay.

> Write an essay using all the notes and give the reasons for your point of view.
> It is better to keep up to date by reading newspapers, rather than blogs and websites.
> Do you agree?
>
> **Notes**
> Write about:
> 1 professional journalism
>   *years of training / quality*
> 2 specialist news
>   *free access on internet / not all contributors are experts*
> 3 ……………………………… (your own idea)

**6** Add one or two points to express your own idea, then write your answer to the question in 140–190 words. Use your notes and give reasons for your point of view.

Making headlines

# 18 Start up

## VOCABULARY  The world of work

**1** Add vowels to complete the phrases about work.

1  B..... N G  Y..... R  .... W N  B.... S S
2  C R..... .... T .... V ....
3  F L.... X .... B L....  W.... R K.... N G  H..... .... R S
4  M.... N..... .... L  W.... R K
5  .... P P.... R T.... N.... T..... .... S  F.... R  F.... R..... .... G N  T R.... V .... L
6  P.... R S.... N..... L L Y  R.... W.... R D.... N G
7  P R.... F.... S S..... .... N.... L  J.... B
8  T.... K.... .... T.... M..... .... F F
9  W.... L L-P..... .... D
10  W.... R K.... N G  S H.... F T S

**2** Complete the sentences with the phrases from exercise 1.

1  I'd rather get a job in an office than do ................................................. .
2  When I leave school I don't want to work for anybody – I'm more interested in ................................................. .
3  I don't want a strict nine-to-five job – I'm looking for something with ................................................. .
4  My job isn't very ................................................., so I can't afford any expensive holidays.
5  I don't get much money for my work, but I love it because it's so ................................................. .
6  I want to see the world, so I'm looking for a job with ................................................. .
7  My father's used to ................................................. – one week he does 6.00 to 2.00, and the next week 2.00 to 10.00.
8  Laura wants to do a ................................................. when she leaves school, like being a doctor or lawyer.
9  Not many jobs allow you to ................................................. when you want, because they like you to be there!
10  I'm not that interested in money, but I'd love to have a ................................................. job, where I can use my artistic skills.

**3** Choose a phrase to describe either the person or the type of work they are looking for.

1  Suraya doesn't particularly want to earn a lot of money but she wants a job that she finds satisfying.
  ................................................
2  Umit is very independent and he finds working for other people very difficult.
  ................................................
3  Anna would like a job that she can fit around looking after her children.
  ................................................
4  Steve has studied foreign languages and he'd like to use them in his work.
  ................................................
5  Jack likes to use his hands.
  ................................................
6  Carla has a good imagination and she likes designing things.
  ................................................

## READING

**1** Do students in your country work in the summer? What kind of jobs do they do?

................................................
................................................

**2** Read the web page quickly. Does a or b best describe its purpose?

a  to show the experiences of students who work during the summer
b  to advise students what kind of summer work would be suitable for them

**3** Match the titles with the paragraphs.

1  Manual work  .......
2  Youth camps  .......
3  Shop work  .......
4  Office work  .......
5  Work experience  .......
6  Festivals  .......

Unit 18

# SUMMER JOBS FOR STUDENTS

**A** ..........................................
This I feel should be the top-rated job for the summer. Not only is it fun – you get to work indoors and outdoors, you get to play with kids, you get to make new friends, sleep in a tent, and best of all you're getting paid for having a laugh! What else could you ask for? It's great experience and it looks good on your CV. The best part is, you're almost guaranteed a place the next year if they feel you were good. Also, some of them take place every holiday – not just summer.

**B** ..........................................
Who doesn't love these?! Wouldn't it be the best job if you worked at one? Imagine free music, you get to see the celebrities, enjoy the music, have fun, get paid and so on. If this sounds like your kind of thing, why don't you look into it? Look online on the popular student jobs site *Just Jobs 4 Students*. Another idea would be to apply to event staff agencies that send their staff to these events. Just be careful you're not tempted to spend all your earnings before you go home!

**C** ..........................................
It might not be your cup of tea but some people like the security of a nine-to-five job. If this is for you, the best bet for the summer would be a temporary desk job (there's always the possibility of it being a permanent one when you leave school if you like it enough, do your job well and the company want to keep you). The easiest and best way to get such work in the summer is to go through an agency. That doesn't mean you can't find jobs by yourself by looking online or through your local newspaper, but it just takes the stress out as the agency do it all for you and find a job that best suits your needs.

**D** ..........................................
Some people might want to work with their hands if they live in the countryside – or just for the sake of doing it. If you know you don't like this kind of physical work, don't do it. If you want to do it, ask around locally, check online, in newspapers on university career websites, etc. I remember last year seeing an advert for strawberry picking in France: you get to travel, camp, earn money and pick strawberries! That would have been fun. There's no limit to what you can do.

**E** ..........................................
Most people go down this route. Working in the High Street does seem attractive and simple but it can be quite hard, and sometimes not worth the money. The best advice for retail jobs would be to apply early. You should start seeing adverts for your favourite stores from late April/early May time, but some take on staff earlier so they can train them. As soon as you see signs (and keep your eyes open for them!), start applying! The earlier you get your CV in and bother them, the more of a chance you have.

**F** ..........................................
This would mainly be for university students who are looking for experience in their chosen field or course. First, internships – unpaid jobs done just for the experience – are hard to obtain and competitive. You have to apply as soon as you discover the opening because there are loads of students and non-students looking for an advantage and an internship is the best way forward for them. Most internships tend to be unpaid but they are valuable. So make sure you apply as soon as you can.

**4 According to the web page, which kind of job:**
1 does not pay at all? ..........................
2 offers opportunities to work at other times of the year? ..........................
3 is best to let someone else find for you? ..........................
4 might tempt you to spend your money before you go home? ..........................
5 offers the opportunity to work in another country? ..........................
6 is more difficult than you might think? ..........................

## Word profile *balance*

**Match the sentences to the correct definition of *balance* below.**

1 The gymnast lost her **balance** and crashed to the ground. ........
2 My account **balance** is a bit low at the moment, so I need to find a job. ........
3 Can you **balance** on your head? ........
4 We need to have a **balance** between our working life and our leisure. ........
5 On **balance**, I think I'd prefer to work in an office, rather than do a manual job. ........

a when the weight is spread to avoid falling over
b when the correct amount of importance is given to two or more things
c the amount of money that you have in your bank account
d to be in a position where you will not fall to either side
e after considering all the facts about something

## GRAMMAR  Uses of verb + -ing

**1** Correct the spelling of the *-ing* form where necessary.

1. I am *writting* to apply for a job in your company. ...................
2. I keep *forgeting* to send you that photo from our holiday. ...................
3. Do you admit *useing* the answer key when you do your homework? ...................
4. *Running* is very good exercise. ...................
5. He spends a lot of time *studing* in his bedroom. ...................
6. What are you *planing* to do when you leave school? ...................
7. Which TV documentary are you *referring* to? ...................
8. My uncle, *beeing* a keen sportsman, is very fit. ...................

**2** Complete the sentences with the *-ing* form of the verbs below.

| apply | arrive | do | feel | move |
|---|---|---|---|---|
| play | try | wait | watch | work |

1. Stella's been ........................... as a waitress in this café for most of the summer.
2. ........................... for summer jobs is not my idea of fun, but I have to do it!
3. Dan spends a lot of time ........................... on his Xbox when he should be studying.
4. Our football coach, ........................... to get us to train harder, offered to buy us all burgers and chips if we won the match.
5. Why do you always insist on ........................... ten minutes early for every class?
6. I don't really enjoy ........................... reality TV shows, but everyone at school talks about them.
7. Jodie's mother is thinking of ........................... to Canada to work as a translator.
8. I haven't been ........................... very well recently, so I haven't done any work on the project.
9. ........................... for the bus in the freezing cold, Jack decided it was time to get himself a new bike.
10. I don't mind ........................... exercise in the gym, but I'd rather go out for a long walk by the river.

**3** Complete the sentences about you. Use the *-ing* form of a verb.

1. Sometimes I dream about ........................... .
2. I can't live without ........................... .
3. I'm looking forward to ........................... .
4. I don't enjoy ........................... .
5. I've been ........................... for years.
6. ........................... makes me feel ill.

**4** Correct the mistakes in these sentences or put a tick (✓) by any you think are correct.

1. I write this letter to say thank you for your hospitality. ...................
2. Everyone panicked and started running towards the exit. ...................
3. I don't mind to work hard and I feel good when I use my time efficiently. ...................
4. I would prefer working with animals instead of helping in an office. ...................

## VOCABULARY  Word pairs

**1** Make eight word pair phrases.

| 1 | more |  | less |
| 2 | round |  | over |
| 3 | more | and | later |
| 4 | sooner | or | two |
| 5 | now |  | then |
| 6 | one |  | more |
| 7 | up |  | round |
| 8 | over |  | down |

1. ...........................
2. ...........................
3. ...........................
4. ...........................
5. ...........................
6. ...........................
7. ...........................
8. ...........................

**2** Choose word pairs from exercise 1 to replace the bold words. You may have to add a word.

1. I enjoy going out for a meal **occasionally**.
   ...........................
2. There are **approximately** 100 employees at this company.
   ...........................
3. It's getting **increasingly** difficult to find a job these days.
   ...........................
4. The temperature has been **rising and falling** all summer – I never know what to wear!
   ...........................
5. Keep trying – I'm sure you'll find what you want **eventually**.
   ...........................
6. We have **a few** problems with the new system, but it's okay on the whole.
   ...........................
7. We tried **repeatedly** to call you, but you never answered.
   ...........................
8. I cycled **continuously in circles in** the park this afternoon so now I'm exhausted!
   ...........................

## LISTENING

**1** Read the sentences below quickly. What is Tonya's talk about?

.................................................................................

Tonya studied (1) .............................. and Spanish at university.
After university, Tonya worked as a (2) .............................. in Portugal.
Tonya was informed by her (3) .............................. about the job at Happy Planet.
Tonya became the director's assistant after working at the company for (4) .............................. months.
Tonya's boss writes about (5) .............................. every week in a newspaper.
It was the quality of the (6) .............................. which she wrote that led to her current job.
Tonya recently enjoyed attending a (7) .............................. in New York.
Tonya often has to deal with (8) .............................. who ask for financial help.
In the future, Tonya hopes to be a (9) .............................. of online videos.
Tonya advises that (10) .............................. is essential if you want to become a travel writer.

### EXAM TIPS

**Listening Part 2**
- Read the sentences first to get the main idea of the listening.
- Make sure the words you put in the gaps fit the sentence grammatically.
- Answer every question, even if you are not sure of the exact words.

**2** Look at each gap in the notes above. Guess what kind of information from the list below is needed to fill the gap. (Two items from the list are used twice.)

|  | Gap(s) |
|---|---|
| an event | ............... |
| a job | ............... |
|  | ............... |
| a topic | ............... |
| a kind of text | ............... |
| a subject of study | ............... |
| a personal quality | ............... |
| a person/organisation | ............... |
|  | ............... |
| a number | ............... |

**3** Look at each gap in the notes again. Work out what kind of word is needed to fill each gap.

|  | Gap(s) |
|---|---|
| number | ............... |
| singular noun | ............... |
|  | ............... |
|  | ............... |
|  | ............... |
| plural noun | ............... |
|  | ............... |
| uncountable noun | ............... |
|  | ............... |

**4** ▶10 🔴 You will hear a woman called Tonya, who works for a travel website, talking to some students about her job. For questions 1–10, complete the sentences with a word or short phrase.

# 19 Points of view

## VOCABULARY  Opinions and beliefs

**1** Match the words and phrases with the definitions.

1. firmly believe in
2. there is no doubt
3. hard to deny
4. be convinced by
5. as far as X is concerned
6. bear in mind
7. go along with
8. be in favour of
9. to my mind
10. be totally against
11. suspect
12. your view on

a. approve or support a plan or idea
b. be confident that something is good
c. be persuaded
d. remember or consider something
e. in my opinion
f. it is certain
g. in X's opinion
h. think that something is probably true
i. disagree entirely with
j. your opinion of
k. difficult to disprove/disagree with
l. agree with

1 ......  2 ......  3 ......  4 ......  5 ......  6 ......
7 ......  8 ......  9 ......  10 ......  11 ......  12 ......

**2** Complete the sentences with words from exercise 1.

1. He wasn't ..................... by my arguments.
2. That, ..................... , is not a practical suggestion.
3. I hope his age ..................... totally ..................... him in the election.
4. Do you have a ..................... the government's youth policy?
5. We don't often agree, but I'd ..................... you there!
6. There ..................... that Simon has worked very hard on this project.
7. ..................... concerned, you can do what you want.
8. Are you ..................... of compulsory voting in elections?

### EP Word profile *mind*

Complete the sentences with the words below.

| bear | crossed | have | put | to | two |

1. If you are in ..................... minds about something, you are having difficulty making a choice.
2. I'd like you to ..................... in mind that you only have one chance to do this.
3. If you ..................... your mind to it, you will almost certainly succeed.
4. I ..................... an open mind about most things.
5. It has never even ..................... my mind that I do not drink enough water.
6. You should, ..................... my mind, have been able to persuade Marco to come with us.

## READING

### EXAM TIPS

**Reading and Use of English Part 5**
- Read the whole text quickly to get an idea of what it is about.
- Read through the questions and ABCD options carefully.
- Underline the parts of the text where you find the correct answer.
- Be careful about choosing an option that has the same words as the text – this won't always lead you to the correct answer.

**1** 🔴 You are going to read an article about two systems of thought. For questions 1–6, choose the answer (A, B, C or D) which you think fits best according to the text.

1. What does the author say about our ability to predict people's behaviour?
   A We should have more confidence in it.
   B It gets more accurate with age.
   C We are quite bad at it.
   D It depends on our mood.

2. According to the author, modern advertising succeeds by
   A accessing our prehistoric mind.
   B appealing to our selfish nature.
   C taking advantage of our fears.
   D causing us to react in a safe way.

3. What does the author say *system 2* is good for?
   A coming up with creative ideas
   B concentrating for long periods
   C performing difficult mental tasks
   D dealing with several problems at the same time

4. The author compares *system 2* to an actor because
   A it pretends to be something it is not.
   B it lacks an understanding of its role.
   C it has little connection with reality.
   D its purpose is to hide the truth.

5. What does 'this' refer to in line 38?
   A a surprisingly good decision
   B an unexpected sports win
   C a complex calculation
   D a clever plan

6. How does the author feel about the future of neuroscience?
   A confident that it will never answer all questions
   B annoyed that it is trying to learn too much
   C hopeful that it will help improve our lives
   D worried that it will become too powerful

# TWO SYSTEMS OF THOUGHT

How good are we at predicting what people will do? What magazine will they buy, what music will they download or what shoes will they choose for a party? Probably not nearly as good as we think. When it comes to human behaviour, the brain is shown to have two different approaches to thinking. So it doesn't matter how old you are or how confident you're feeling, it's all about what mood the brain is in!

A common thought process is the automatic and fast approach which helps us to react quickly in dangerous situations. This is known as *system 1* and dates back to the times of our prehistoric ancestors, who lived with a natural awareness of the dangers around them – bad weather, falling rocks and trees, and threatening animals. Nowadays, we still have the ability to react so rapidly and naturally to situations that it can feel like you're not thinking at all. Have you ever found yourself giving in to temptation and unable to say 'no' to buying that new jacket in the window? This is because *system 1* is in control – a human characteristic which the world of advertising likes to make the most of!

*System 2* is the opposite. It's a slow thought process that requires us to pay attention and concentrate – for example, when doing a complex mathematical sum. This way of thinking helps us to make sensible long-term decisions like choosing which university to study at, or what type of car to buy. The problem is that *system 2* often starts to feel boring and so *system 1* takes over. How often have you put down your homework or put off doing important jobs to go on Facebook or watch a TV soap?

We like to think that we go through life mainly using *system 2*. As individuals, we are in control, always taking sensible and logical decisions. *System 1* type thoughts are reserved for special occasions when we can afford to relax a little – on holiday perhaps. However, this first system actually plays more of a secondary role in our lives, with the latter taking the main stage. *System 2* behaves like a supporting actor in a film, who believes himself to be the leading character, but actually has little idea of what's going on!

Sometimes it's *system 1* that makes the right decision but *system 2* that gets it wrong. For example, professional sports teams put a lot of effort into a game plan but often it's the unconscious human wish to do something differently that leads to a spectacular goal. **This** can also lead to the common mistaken idea that your successful decisions demonstrate your skill and talent, when in fact they were just luck.

Perhaps one day scientists will be able to predict what decisions people will make by measuring brain activity. In one study, volunteers were monitored with brain-scanning equipment. They were asked to press either a left or a right button whenever they wanted. The researchers found they could predict which button the volunteers would press up to seven seconds before it happened – your brain seems to know what it will do before you do! Some scientists say our brains are just machines and we are not really in control of what's going on. Let's hope they're wrong! It's one thing to be able to tell which of two buttons a person will press, but I don't like the idea that science could one day tell me what decisions I will make in my life before I've even had the chance to make them!

**2** Find words in the text which mean the following.

1 a way of doing something (paragraph 2) ..............
2 a feeling that you want to do or have something, although you know you shouldn't (paragraph 2) ..............
3 a typical or noticeable quality of someone or something (paragraph 2) ..............
4 a person, especially when considered separately and not as part of a group (paragraph 4) ..............
5 the second of two people, things or groups previously mentioned (paragraph 4) ..............

## GRAMMAR  Subject–verb agreement

**1** Complete the sentences with the correct form of the verbs in brackets.

1. A number of people ............................. (ask) me about the geography field trip already.
2. The process for selecting students for the quiz teams ............................. (be) now in place.
3. All of the students ............................. (be) waiting in the hall.
4. Having more than three children per family ............................. (contribute) to global over-population.
5. No one ............................. (understand) how consciousness arose.
6. One of the scientists in the team ............................. (be) only 20 years old.
7. The government ............................. (plan) to increase funding for science research.
8. Politics ............................. (be) not a very interesting subject for me.
9. Everyone in the class ............................. (take) the English exam next week.
10. Both of Keira's sisters ............................. (look) very much like her.

**2** Choose the correct form of the verb. If both are possible, choose them both.

> Hi Alan
> I'm sorry to say that not much progress ¹ *has / have* been made in finding people to take part in our psychology experiment. Plenty of people ² *has / have* said it sounds interesting, but nobody ³ *has / have* offered to help yet, although a couple of my students ⁴ *is / are* thinking about it. I think taking part in an experiment ⁵ *frightens / frighten* them. Even my family ⁶ *isn't / aren't* keen, and I don't want to make them feel guilty, so I don't push them. I'm particularly disappointed that the science club ⁷ *hasn't / haven't* even replied to our request. I'll let you know if any more news ⁸ *arrives / arrive* tomorrow, but I'm not very hopeful.
> Best,
> Tina

**3** 👁 Correct the mistakes in these sentences or put a tick (✓) by any you think are correct.

1. I do not have many news to tell you.
   ............................
2. The food at both of the restaurant are different.
   ............................
3. The atmosphere in both of them is informal, calm and friendly. ............................
4. If you visit some friends everybody have a computer at home. ............................

## VOCABULARY  Plural nouns

**1** Complete the word puzzle, using the clues below.

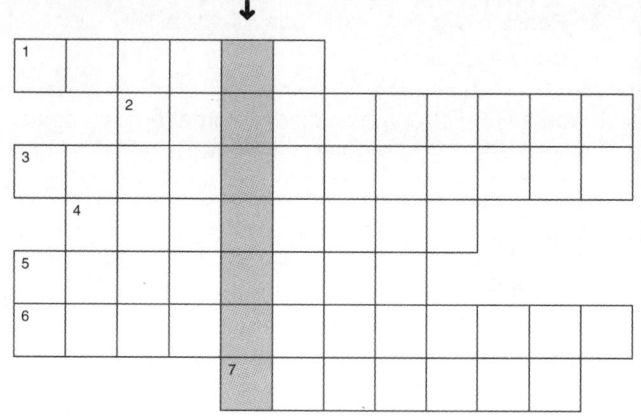

1. the words of a song
2. what a person owns
3. the area around a place
4. the list at the start of a book which tells you what the book contains
5. the images on a computer screen
6. food and drinks
7. all the money you have kept for the future

Word reading down (↓): ............................

**2** Complete the sentences with words from exercise 1.

1. Have you seen the latest Nintendo game? The ............................ are amazing!
2. We will be serving ............................ at eleven o'clock.
3. I would sing the song for you, but I've forgotten the ............................ .
4. Before I buy a book, I always read the ............................ page.
5. This town is very nice, and so are its ............................ .
6. Your ............................ are all wet. What have you been doing?
7. Please take all your ............................ with you when you leave the train.
8. I spent all my ............................ on a new bicycle.

Unit 19

# WRITING  A review (2)

See Prepare to write box, Student's Book pages 79 and 101.

**1** Read the Writing Part 2 task and answer the questions below.

> You have seen a notice on an international students' website asking for reviews of games or apps.
>
> > **Reviews wanted!**
> > We are looking for reviews of computer games or apps for teens. Send us a review of a game or app you know well, telling us
> > - the aim or purpose of the game/app
> > - who it is aimed at
> > - about its controls and graphics
> > - whether you would recommend it
>
> Write your **review**.

1 Where will the review appear? ......................

2 Who will read the review? ..........................

3 Should the language in the review be formal or informal? ..........................

**2** Read the game review below. Did the writer answer all the questions in the task? Ignore the gaps.

> The new *Speed Racer* game came out last week. ¹....... Like all racing games, the aim is to get to the finish line before anybody else does. What makes *Speed Racer* different from all the others is the control you get over the kind of vehicle you're driving. In fact, half the fun of the game comes before the actual race – when you build the car of your dreams! Once you've constructed your dream car, ²....... ten different tracks to race on. I thought the controls responded well and they were simple, but not so simple as to make the game easy to win. ³....... there's loads of room to improve your skills. I still can't do better than third place on track 10!
>
> The graphics are the one thing that lets the game down a bit, but the game play is so smooth that you don't really mind in the end. Realism isn't everything, after all. *Speed Racer* is ⁴......., and definitely worth buying, especially if you're into racing. Keep an eye out for it!

## EXAM TIPS

**Writing Part 2 (a review)**
- You can make your review quite informal.
- Think about using contractions, questions, exclamations, phrasal verbs and informal vocabulary.

**3** The review is informal. Find at least one example of the following features of informal language.

1 contractions ..........................

2 exclamations ..........................

3 phrasal verbs ..........................

4 informal vocabulary ..........................

**4** Look at the pairs of phrases. Match them to the gaps and choose the more informal phrase for each gap.

**A** a  you get to choose from
    b  you are given the option of

**B** a  Indeed,
    b  Believe me,

**C** a  The game is of outstanding quality.
    b  And what a game it is!

**D** a  a really cool buy
    b  an excellent purchase

**5** Read the task in exercise 1 again and write your own review. Use 140–190 words.

# 20 Speak up

## VOCABULARY Idioms

**1** Match the two halves of the phrases to make idioms.

1 break .......     a track of something
2 break .......     b an eye for
3 take .......     c the ice
4 be .......     d a pain
5 be .......     e your mind
6 cross .......     f someone's heart
7 have .......     g your breath away
8 lose .......     h a piece of cake

**2** Complete the sentences below with the correct forms of the idioms.

1 Oh, stop .............................................. – you're really annoying me!
2 That exam .............................................. – I'm sure I got 100%.
3 It never .............................................. that we might not be able to get tickets for this concert. I'm so disappointed.
4 Do you know any good activities to .............................................. when a new class begins?
5 I always take my aunt with me when I go shopping because she .............................................. a bargain!
6 It .............................................. to see you so unhappy – is there anything I can do to help?
7 When we reached the top of the mountain, the amazing view .............................................. .
8 I'm sorry, I .............................................. what the teacher is talking about.

**3** Complete the second sentence so that it has a similar meaning to the first sentence, using the word in brackets.

1 Watching my cat grow old made me sad. (heart)
It .............................. to watch my cat grow old.
2 Getting into the house through the back window was very easy. (cake)
It .............................. to get into the house through the back window.
3 Have you ever thought about buying a bicycle? (crossed)
Has .............................. to buy a bicycle?
4 When I first saw London from the air the view really amazed me. (breath)
The view .......................... when I first saw London from the air.
5 Starting with a game is a good way to make everyone feel relaxed at a party. (ice)
A good way ............................ at a party is to start with a game.

## READING

**1** Read the title of the article and the first paragraph quickly. Where do you think the article is from?

a a poster    b a newspaper    c a textbook

### EXAM TIPS

**Reading and Use of English Part 6**
- Read the text and the sentences A–G for their general meaning.
- Look for links in the sentences before and after each gap in the text.
- Underline the important words and phrases in the sentences A–G and look for linking words.
- Read through the whole text with your answers in place to check it makes sense.

**2** 🔴 You are going to read an article about an invented language. Six sentences have been removed from the article. Choose from the sentences A–G the one which fits each gap (1–6). There is one extra sentence which you do not need to use.

A It is also the 29th most used language on Wikipedia ahead of Danish and Arabic.
B The native language is regarded by many there as already performing the role aimed at by Esperanto.
C One is that everyone speaks English and the other is that no one speaks Esperanto.
D The language was created by Lazar Zamenhof in 1887 in response to linguistic divisions in his native Poland.
E One of the main aims of the campaign is to make the language part of the national curriculum in as many countries as possible.
F Actors, businesspeople, scientists, artists and novelists – the breadth of Esperanto's appeal cannot be underestimated.
G According to the Esperanto Society, there are only around two million speakers worldwide.

## ESPERANTO SPEAKERS LAUNCH A NEW DRIVE TO GAIN INTERNATIONAL RECOGNITION

More than 1,000 enthusiastic campaigners from all over the world will gather in a conference hall in Iceland tomorrow to launch their latest attempt to get international recognition for the language they can all speak. Friday is Esperanto Day – set up to promote the language which was invented 125 years ago in an attempt to bring different cultures closer together by removing language barriers.

It has, it would only be fair to point out, had an up and down history since then. ☐ 1 However, it does appear to be gaining popularity among the young. The International Youth Congress of Esperanto has a conference every year, with recent attendance figures of up to 500.

Internationally, around 600 primary and secondary schools in 28 countries teach it and it is officially taught in 150 universities, although it is not recognised as a modern foreign language for national curriculum purposes in England. ☐ 2 A spokeswoman for the Department of Education in the UK said, 'It would be very difficult for a school to teach Esperanto as part of the current national curriculum as there are no Esperanto literary texts and no culture to interact with.'

☐ 3 He believed that language barriers fostered conflict, and therefore set about promoting it as a 'neutral' second language that had no political history. He just wanted people to get along. In the 1920s, there were attempts at the League of Nations – the organisation which became the United Nations – to make it the language of international relations but these were resisted.

The delegates at the conference on Friday, who will be greeting each other with a cheerful *saluton* (hello), would like to see it play a more important role in the workings of institutions like the UN and the European Union. 'There are two urban myths about the international language problem,' said Brian Barker of the Esperanto Society. '☐ 4 Both are untrue and both need to be challenged.'

The language has not been without heavyweight supporters. ☐ 5 Millionaire financier George Soros and *Star Trek* actor William Shatner (who even starred in a movie filmed entirely in Esperanto) have promoted it, and others who have spoken the language include J.R.R.Tolkien and Leo Tolstoy.

Supporters of the language argue that it is easy to learn and understand because it has a fairly simple grammatical structure. They point out that in its 'short history of 125 years' it has established itself in the top 100 of languages worldwide (out of a total of 6,800).
☐ 6 In addition, to argue against the Government's point about the lack of literary texts, they say there is a 'rich body' of more than 50,000 titles which have either been translated into or written in Esperanto.

There is no shortage of campaigners ready to promote the language, therefore, although whether it will become more widespread in future remains to be seen.

---

**3 Choose the correct ending to each sentence.**

1 According to the writer, Esperanto has *had varying success / been unfairly criticised / improved relations between countries*.
2 Esperanto is not officially taught in English schools because *it lacks cultural depth / very few people speak it / English is the international language*.
3 In lines 24–5 'fostered conflict' means *made education difficult / interfered with politics / caused social problems*.
4 Supporters of Esperanto claim that *many famous people speak it / it has achieved a lot in a short time / soon everyone will understand it*.

**4 Find words in the text which mean the following.**

1 come together (paragraph 1) ...........................
2 the group of subjects studied in a school, college, etc. (paragraph 3) ...........................
3 opposed (paragraph 4) ...........................
4 supported and encouraged (paragraph 6) ...........................
5 connected with books and reading (paragraph 7) ...........................

---

**EP Word profile** *standard*

Match the use of the word *standard* in these sentences with the definitions.

1 We expect our politicians to have high **standards**, but we are often disappointed.
2 The **standard** of the cooking oil you used wasn't great; that's why the food tastes bad.
3 Is there a **standard** procedure to follow when something like this happens?

a a level of quality, especially a level that is acceptable
b a level of behaviour, especially a level that is acceptable
c usual rather than special, especially when thought of as being correct or acceptable

## GRAMMAR  Determiners

**1  Complete the sentences with *a, an, the* or – (no article)**

1. We haven't been to ............ theatre in Park Street for ............ ages.
2. 'What did you have for ............ breakfast?' 'I ate ............ eggs that were in ............ fridge.'
3. I learned to speak ............ French when I was ............ engineering student in Paris.
4. Unfortunately, ............ film was ............ disaster, and we left ............ cinema halfway through.
5. Do you have ............ explanation for ............ terrible mess in this room?
6. Why is she speaking with ............ foreign accent? I thought she was ............ native English speaker.
7. ............ best thing about this book is that it makes ............ really nice coffee mat.
8. London is ............ great city to live in if you like ............ noise and ............ traffic.

**2  Choose the correct answer.**

1. *Much / Plenty of* people around the world speak Esperanto.
2. We've had *a few / a bit of* difficulty collecting all the data.
3. There is a small *number / amount* of students who haven't finished their project.
4. I'm sorry, I don't have *many / some* tickets left.
5. This job is going to take a large *number / amount* of effort for very *little / few* reward.
6. I don't want *a lot of / many* food tonight, thanks – I'm going training.
7. *Any / Several* of our members have expressed an interest in the trip.
8. Tara has *plenty / a few* questions she would like to ask you.
9. I can give you a hand quickly, but I really haven't got *some / a lot of* time.
10. *Little / Some* native American languages are still spoken in North America.

**3  Complete the sentences with *(a) little* or *(a) few*.**

1. I tried, but it was ............................ use.
2. I'm worried about my sister, who has ............................ friends.
3. Eventually, ............................ diners entered the restaurant.
4. This soup needs ............................ salt and pepper.
5. Surprisingly, ............................ children in the school could spell correctly.
6. Please be quick. We have ............................ time to waste.
7. I've got ............................ time now if you want to talk about the homework.
8. There were ............................ students at the lecture – not the whole group but enough.

**4  Correct the mistakes in these sentences or put a tick (✓) by any you think are correct.**

1. I hope you will have a great fun. ............................
2. Can you imagine the school where you can study only the subjects you enjoy? ............................
3. Furthermore, I am a very reliable and responsible person. ............................
4. However, not much people like to read a book. ............................
5. I was really happy to spend few days with you. ............................

## VOCABULARY  Commonly confused words

**1  Choose the correct answer.**

1. I love trains – they are my favourite ....... of transport.
   a  means    b  journey    c  way
2. Excuse me. Do you know the ....... to the airport?
   a  means    b  journey    c  way
3. The best ....... to learn something is to practise it.
   a  means    b  journey    c  way
4. Is there a slight ....... that you might come and visit us this month?
   a  opportunity    b  possibility    c  happening
5. That was a very ....... film. I couldn't stop laughing!
   a  funny    b  sad    c  fun
6. Did you get the ....... to talk to the director about your ideas?
   a  opportunity    b  possibility    c  happening
7. We went to the park, but it wasn't much ....... .
   a  funny    b  happy    c  fun
8. I ....... my leg during a football match.
   a  harmed    b  injured    c  damaged
9. Be careful you don't ....... my camera.
   a  harm    b  injure    c  damage
10. Don't worry, the snake isn't poisonous – it won't ....... you.
    a  harm    b  injure    c  damage
11. Can you ....... how much money I have in my pocket?
    a  know    b  observe    c  guess
12. I learned how to play chess by ....... my dad play with his friend.
    a  knowing    b  observing    c  guessing

**2  Answer the questions for you.**

1. What is your favourite means of transport?
2. What do you find funny?
3. Do you usually know all the answers to the exercises, or do you guess some?
4. What is the longest journey you have ever made?
5. Have you ever missed an important opportunity?
6. Have you ever injured yourself?

## LISTENING

**1** Look at the questions on the right. Underline the main points in each question.

### EXAM TIPS

**Listening Part 1**
- Read the question carefully before you listen.
- If you are still not sure of the answer after one listening, underline the key words in the question before you listen again.
- Use the second listening to reject the options which you think are wrong.

**2** ▶11 You will hear people talking in eight different situations. Listen to the first extract and answer question 1.

**3** Now look at the extract and underline the part which leads you to the correct answer.

**Girl:** So, what did you think of your first rugby match?
**Boy:** It was a bit confusing, actually. I still don't understand the rules.
**Girl:** So you didn't enjoy it? That's a shame.
**Boy:** Oh, I wouldn't have missed it for the world! I just didn't follow what was going on, that's all. But the players were obviously very good at what they do.
**Girl:** So, would you come again?
**Boy:** Yes, but I'll be sure to eat before we go next time. I was starving for most of the game. It was hard to concentrate.
**Girl:** OK, next time we'll have lunch at the clubhouse restaurant. It's very good.

**4** ▶11 Listen to all of the extracts and match them with the pictures.

a  b  c  d  e  f  g  h

**5** ▶11 Now listen again. You will hear people talking in seven more situations. For questions 2–8, choose the best answer (A, B or C).

1  You hear two people talking about a rugby match they've just seen.
   How does the boy feel about it?
   **A** happy to have experienced it
   **B** unimpressed by the skills of the players
   **C** pleased with the quality of the food available

2  You overhear two friends talking about a new café.
   What do they agree is good about it?
   **A** the service
   **B** the prices
   **C** the atmosphere

3  You hear a girl talking about a jacket she bought online.
   What is she complaining about?
   **A** She was sent the wrong size.
   **B** She was charged too much.
   **C** The jacket was delivered too late.

4  You hear a dancer talking about his life and work.
   What is he trying to explain?
   **A** why his mother was so successful
   **B** his reasons for becoming a dancer
   **C** the similarities between classical and modern dance

5  You hear two friends talking about going on holiday.
   Why is the girl worried about going on holiday?
   **A** She might lose her role in the school play.
   **B** She won't be able to afford to pay for anything.
   **C** She doesn't have confidence in the other drama club members.

6  You hear an interview with a young businessman.
   What is his business?
   **A** hiring out motorcycles
   **B** repairing motorcycles
   **C** selling advertising space

7  You overhear a boy telling a friend about his summer job at a sports camp for kids.
   How is he feeling?
   **A** surprised at how tired he is
   **B** upset at his students' behaviour
   **C** relieved that his approach worked

8  You hear a review of a TV documentary which is based on a book.
   What is the reviewer's opinion of the documentary?
   **A** It is disappointing.
   **B** It is better than the book.
   **C** It contains too much information.

# Acknowledgements

Development of this publication has made use of the Cambridge English Corpus, a multi-billion word collection of spoken and written English. It includes the Cambridge Learner Corpus, a unique collection of candidate exam answers. Cambridge University Press has built up the Cambridge English Corpus to provide evidence about language use that helps to produce better language teaching materials.

This product is informed by English Profile, a Council of Europe-endorsed research programme that is providing detailed information about the language that learners of English know and use at each level of the Common European Framework of Reference (CEFR). For more information, please visit www.englishprofile.org

**The authors and publishers acknowledge the following sources of copyright material and are grateful for the permissions granted. While every effort has been made, it has not always been possible to identify the sources of all the material used, or to trace all copyright holders. If any omissions are brought to our notice, we will be happy to include the appropriate acknowledgements on reprinting.**

Aquila Magazine for the text on p. 5 from 'Read it!', previously published in *AQUILA magazine*, March 2013: https://www.aquila.co.uk. All rights reserved, New Leaf Publishing 2012–2014. Reproduced with permission; The Guardian for the text on p.17 adapted from 'Experience: I've been to the quietest place on Earth' by George Mickleson Foy, *The Guardian* 18/5/2012. Copyright Guardian News & Media Limited 2012; Aquila Magazine for the text on p. 21 adapted from 'Circus History', previously published in AQUILA magazine, July/August 2013. https://www.aquila.co.uk. All rights reserved, New Leaf Publishing 2012–2014. Reproduced with permission; Encyclopaedia Britannica for the text on p. 21 adapted from 'Colosseum'. Adapted with permission from *Encyclopaedia Britannica*. Copyright © 2014 by Encyclopaedia Britannica, Inc; Aquila Magazine for the text on p. 25 adapted from 'Blissfully Boring: The joy of doing nothing', previously published in AQUILA magazine, April 2013 https://www.aquila.co.uk. All rights reserved, New Leaf Publishing 2012–2014. Reproduced with permission; The Associated Press for the text on p. 29 (C) adapted from 'Book's success surprises teen author' by Deepti Hajela, 24/4/2004, *The Associated Press*. Used with permission of The Associated Press Copyright © 2014. All rights reserved; The Weather Channel for the text on p. 33 adapted from 'Masdar City: The Sustainable City of the Future' by Eric Zerkel, published 26/3/14. Copyright © The Weather Channel. Reproduced with permission; Jenna Good and WHO Magazine for the text on p. 49 adapted from' Spreading the Love: Juan Mann' by Jenna Good, *WHO Magazine* 301/2008. Reproduced with permission from WHO Magazine and Jenna Good; Professor Andre Spicer for the text on p. 53 adapted from 'What makes a good leader' by Professor Andre Spicer, http://chronicle.com/campusViewpointArticle/What-Makes-a-Good-Leader-/669. Copyright © Andre Spicer, Professor of Organisational Behaviour at Cass Business School, London. Reproduced with permission; Untamed Path.com for the text on p. 57 adapted from 'Defining Ecotourism', by Michael Merg at www.untamedpath.com. Reproduced with permission; Metro for the text on p. 61 (Do we care about charities) adapted from 'Charities losing out thanks to social media 'slacktivism'', *Metro* 11/11/2013. Copyright Associated Newspapers Limited. Reproduced with permission; The Student Room for the text on p. 73 adapted from 'Common Summer jobs for students' http://www.thestudentroom.co.uk/wiki/summer_job_guide_for_students. Copyright © The Student Room 2014 all rights reserved. Reproduced with permission; The Independent for the text on p. 81 adapted from 'Ĉu vi parolas Esperanton? Esperanto speakers launch new drive to gain international recognition' by Richard Garner, *the Independent* 25/7/2013. Copyright © Independent. Reproduced with permission.

## Photo acknowledgements

p. 5: (A) HarperCollins/HarperCollins/Penelope Lively 2011, (B) Little, Brown/Little, Brown UK, (C) Zdenko Basic (illustration)/Mandy Norman (design), (D) Troubador/Troubador Publishing, (E) Orion Publishing Co; p. 7: Rex/Tom Dymond; p. 9: Shutterstock/Syda Productions; p. 10: Shutterstock/Zyankarlo; p. 11: (R) Getty/John Giustina, (1) Shutterstock/Monkey Business Images, (2) Shutterstock/East, (3) Getty/Mark Rose, (4) Shutterstock/TAGSTOCK1; p. 13: Alamy/David Buch Photography ; p. 15: Shutterstock/Susan Schmitz; p. 17: Alamy/ZUMA Press, Inc; p. 19: (a) Getty/Jeannot Olivet, (b) Alamy/Elvele Images Ltd, (c) Shutterstock/Zurijeta, (d) Alamy/Ace Stock Limited, (e) Shutterstock/Maridav; p. 21: (T) Alamy/Larry Lilac, (B) Shutterstock/Georgy Kuryatov; p. 23: Alamy/Everett Collection Historical; p. 24: Getty/Tyler Edwards; p. 25: Getty/Carlos Davila; p. 29: (A) Shutterstock/oliveromg, (B) Shutterstock/Mik Lav, (C) Rex/Ville Myllynen, (D) Alamy/PhotosIndia.com LLC; p. 33: Alamy/Iain Masterton; p. 35: Getty/Twilight Tea Landscape Photography; p. 44: Getty/Joan Vicent Cantó Roig; p. 45: Alamy/Planetpix; p. 49: Alamy/Alex Hinds; p. 53: Shutterstock/Alena Root; p. 55: Alamy/Evan Robinson; p. 57: Getty/Danita Delimont; p. 59: Alamy/Joe Fox; p. 61: Corbis/Andersen Ross/Blend Images; p. 63: Getty/John Eder; p. 64: Getty/Charly Franklin; p. 65: Rex/Snap Stills; p. 67: Shutterstock/Vassamon Anansukkasem; p. 69: (A) Alamy/Radius Images, (B) Alamy/Wavebreakmedia Ltd PH26L, (C) Shutterstock/AVAVA, (D) Shutterstock/Mettus, (E) Shutterstock/solominviktor; p. 71: Corbis/237/Robert Daly/Ocean; p. 72: (L) Getty/Caiaimage/Martin Barraud, (CL) Shutterstock/anyaivanova, (CR) Alamy/Monty Rakusen, (R) Getty/ilbusca p. 75: Getty/Chris Schmidt; p. 77: (T) Shutterstock/Jeff Wasserman, (B) Getty/David Malan; pp. 80–81: Getty/exdez.

Front cover photograph by Ollyy/Shutterstock.

## Illustrations

Rory Walker pp. 6, 18, 27, 31, 34, 37, 41, 42, 60, 78, 83; Mark Duffin p. 79.

**The publishers are grateful to the following contributors:** text design and layouts: emc design Ltd; cover design: Andrew Ward; picture research: emc design Ltd; audio recordings: produced by IH Sound and recorded at DSound, London; edited by Diane Hall and Helen Forrest.